T0345229

CHERRY

Reaktion's Botanical series is the first of its kind, integrating horticultural and botanical writing with a broader account of the cultural and social impact of trees, plants and flowers.

CHERRY

Constance L. Kirker
and Mary Newman

REAKTION BOOKS

*To our husbands, Tom and John, who have been with us
every step of our cherry journey*

Published by
REAKTION BOOKS LTD
Unit 32, Waterside
44–48 Wharf Road
London N1 7UX, UK

www.reaktionbooks.co.uk

First published 2021
Copyright © Constance L. Kirker and Mary Newman 2021

Printed and bound in India by Replika Press Pvt. Ltd

A catalogue record for this book is available from the British Library

ISBN 978 1 78914 282 2

Contents

Cherry blossoms in Fukuoka, Japan.

Introduction

❦

I want to do to you what spring does with the cherry trees

PABLO NERUDA[1]

The appreciation and obvious pleasure gained by simply observing the cherry fruit or its stunning blossoms is universal. Everyone likes cherries, and seemingly no one can resist the beauty of the flowering cherry tree. But what is most fascinating is the range of metaphorical meanings and almost visceral sensations conjured up by both the blossoms and the fruit of this amazing tree.

The ripe, sensuous, irresistible fruit can symbolize such divergent concepts as fertility, innocence and seductiveness. The blossoms can foretell the new beginnings of life in the spring, fertility writ large. They also represent the beautiful, fleeting and fragile quality of life, as well as the sadness of premature death, or sometimes even the Japanese concept of the 'perfect death'.

The cherry can also represent something as fundamental as the letter 'c' in a child's alphabet book, or even the primary colour red. The double-stemmed shape is instantly and universally recognizable, so much so that one of the first food emojis used in social media was of two cherries, symbolizing the situation of being in a relationship. Helena, in Shakespeare's *A Midsummer Night's Dream* (1605), refers to the double cherry as a close relationship:

So we grew together,
Like to a double cherry, seeming parted,
But yet a union in partition;
Two lovely berries moulded on one stem . . .

The seventeenth-century painter Titian, the twentieth-century writer D. H. Lawrence and pop culture figures like humorist Erma Bombeck and graphic artist Andy Warhol are among those who have used the cherry as a symbol in a variety of creative ways. Even if one has never read Bombeck's book *If Life Is a Bowl of Cherries, What Am I Doing in the Pits?*, the sentiment is universally understood. Cherries and their blossoms have been the subject of songs in many cultures, from the Japanese *sakura* songs celebrating the blossoms from as early as the eighth century CE, to the 1866 French song 'Le Temps des cerises' (Cherry Time), and the 1966 'Cherry, Cherry' by singer-songwriter Neil Diamond. The message in the Palme d'Or prize-winning Iranian film *The Taste of Cherry* (1997) is that eating cherries can be one of the small but intense pleasures in life that might even save someone from suicide. In the last scene of Herman Melville's novel *Moby-Dick*, when the ship is in its final battle with the great white whale, second mate Stubb cries out for 'one red cherry ere we die!'

Philosophers have used the image of cherries to explain complex concepts of beauty and, in some cases, reality itself. Scholars have used the fruit-laden cherry branch to explain Kant's concept of pleasure, good and beauty. Kant based his analogy on 'Berkeley's Cherry'. George Berkeley, in *Three Dialogues between Hylas and Philonous* (1713), argues that 'to be' is 'to be perceived', using a cherry as an example:

> I see this cherry, I feel it, I taste it: and I am sure nothing cannot be seen, or felt, or tasted: it is therefore real. Take away the sensations of softness, moisture, redness, tartness, and you take away the cherry, since it is not a being distinct from sensations. A cherry, I say, is nothing but a congeries of sensible impressions, or ideas perceived by various senses.

8

Fruit-laden cherry
branch, Fundão,
Portugal.

In *The Interpretation of Dreams* (1899), Freud used the example of a child's dream of eating cherries to characterize dreams as a form of wish fulfilment, embodying the core of Freudian theory.

So powerful is the word 'cherry' that it creates a universally descriptive image in one's mind that helps to define terms and expressions that have little or nothing to do with the fruit or tree: cherry tomatoes, cherry-picking, cherry bomb, bowl of cherries, cherry on top. To lose one's cherry is but one of many sexual phrases from urban slang which actually have their origins in sixteenth-century poetry.

Cherry can also refer to something new or unused, or to a novice. In contemporary slang, a cherry refers to a first offender. During the Vietnam War, aviators lost their cherry after taking their first hits by enemy fire. There is even a meaning for 'cherry' in ten-pin bowling: the striking down of only the forward pin or pins in attempting to make a spare. Chapter Five examines cherry imagery as an element in mythology and religion, as well as in the arts and popular culture.

We begin the book with the origins of the cherry tree, its distribution around the world and the ways it is cultivated. We look at how the fruit is harvested, processed, marketed and turned into various food products. Cherries and cherry bark are used as an ingredient in medicine, and cherries have even been called a superfood because of their antioxidant properties. On the other hand, there are toxins in the leaves, stems, stones (or pits) and bark that can kill people and animals.

But this isn't just a book about the ubiquitous cherry fruit; we also discuss the cherry tree's various components, such as its blossoms, wood, bark, leaves, stones and sap. For example, in the Middle East the kernel of the cherry stone is used as a flavouring for many sweets. In European folklore cherry wood is thought to make excellent magic wands, and a blossoming cherry bough could predict an impending marriage opportunity.

Recognizing the economic value of cherries, tourist departments in cherry-growing regions of countries such as Portugal, France and Italy have created 'cherry routes', from train trips to hiking trails. In Japan a number of historically famous cherry blossom viewing spots can only be reached by boat. The focus of all these events is to capitalize on people's widespread desire to experience cherries as both a blossoming harbinger of spring and a glorious, highly perishable early summer fruit.

This book should be considered a 'cherry route' of sorts. We hope you enjoy the journey. Pun intended, we have cherry-picked the most interesting facts and stories about the cherry from the vast amount of information we uncovered. We look forward to sharing with you the energy, vitality and sense of renewal implied in the lines of Neruda's poem.

Blooming cherry tree, Kodaiji temple, Kyoto, Japan.

'Early Morello' variety in a watercolour by Mary Daisy Arnold,
early 20th century.

one

History, Cultivation and Consumption

Though there are literally hundreds of species, varieties and cultivars of cherries, this book will focus mainly on the six most common and characteristic species. The Japanese flowering cherry (*Prunus serrulata*) is known for its beautiful blossoms, while sweet cherry (*P. avium*) and sour cherry (*P. cerasus*) are commercially important species for human consumption. Chokecherry (*P. virginiana*) is known for its historical pharmacological uses. Mahaleb (*P. mahaleb*) is a unique spice made from the cherry stone. The wood of the American black cherry (*P. serotina*) is highly prized by woodworkers throughout the world.

The classification and origin of cherries is complex and sometimes controversial. From the earliest illustrated herbals to the Medici-commissioned paintings during the Renaissance, many attempts were made to document and identify varieties and clarify the classification process. Prior to photography, one method of precisely documenting the details of particular varieties of cherries was to create wax models. In the late nineteenth century, as major fruit-producing regions in the United States began to flourish, the United States Department of Agriculture (USDA) in Washington, DC, recognized the need for accurate identification of fruits, including the cherry. It commissioned 65 artists to paint watercolour illustrations and create wax models. Creating fruit replicas in wax was universally popular and many examples can be found in institutions around the world.[1] They are fragile and costly to repair. Indeed, in one example thousands of dollars were spent repairing a single cherry stem on one wax model.

More accessible and less fragile than the wax models are the 7,584 watercolours in the USDA collection that have recently been digitalized and made available to the public. One of the top three contributors to this collection, Deborah Griscom Passmore, painted more than 1,000 watercolours of fruit and fruit trees. Interestingly, the USDA provided some of the first professional opportunities for women artists in the early twentieth century. Meticulously and beautifully illustrating the characteristics of the species, varieties and cultivars of cherries, Passmore's paintings have been deemed a national treasure by the USDA.

The complex question of the exact origin and dissemination of cherries, however, remains unresolved. The research suggests that sweet cherries originated in a region south of the Caucasus Mountains between the Caspian and Black Seas, an area including Asia Minor, northern Iraq, Syria and Ukraine.[2] From these origins the cherry spread into western Europe.[3]

There are conflicting opinions concerning the origin of sour cherries, with some researchers suggesting that they came from the same area as sweet cherries, while others propose an area extending from the Adriatic Sea to central Europe, and from the Caspian Sea to northern Europe. It is also possible that the sour cherry was originally a hybrid between the sweet cherry and the ground cherry.[4]

Both sweet and sour cherries were spread beyond their places of origin by birds, humans and other animals. It is known that cultivated cherries were grown in Mesopotamian orchards as early as 722 BCE. The cherry tree was known to the ancient Greeks and Romans. The Greek historian Herodotus (484–425 BCE) mentions a cherry from a tree called *ponticum*. He writes, 'it was the staple diet of a Scythian race called the *Argippaei*, who lived each man beneath his own ponticum tree, and protected the trees from winter frosts by binding thick white felt around them.' The fruit, he states, was strained to

Mosaic design of an unswept floor featuring dropped cherries from a Roman villa of the 2nd century BCE.

form a thick juice called *aschy*, which they drank, and the sediment was formed into cakes.[5]

Pliny and Virgil both described cherry cultivars during Roman times, with Pliny claiming they originated in Asia and were brought to Rome by the Roman general Lucullus in 74 BCE. Pliny may have been referring to the particular 'Pontic' cherry variety, from the *ponticum* cherry tree mentioned by Herodotus.[6]

Pliny also wrote about a sweet cherry called the 'Junian' cherry, which he said 'has a pleasant taste, but only if eaten under its tree, since it is so tender that it cannot stand being transported'.[7] The

Romans expanded cherry cultivation throughout western Europe and into Britain. A legend says that the routes of old Roman roads in Britain can be detected by the presence of wild cherry trees, as Roman legions spat out cherry seeds while marching.[8]

Early Islamic orchards contained cherries among many other types of flowering fruit trees. Caravan merchants traded cherries for other foods and spices. Islamic cities had many gardens, and on the outskirts great orchards were filled with orange, lemon, apple, pomegranate and cherry trees.

In Britain cherry cultivation died out with the fall of the Western Roman Empire in the fifth century CE. However, the fruit was re-introduced following the Norman invasion in 1066 CE, and by the sixteenth century significant cherry cultivation was underway in Kent in the south of England.

In 1585 Jean Morelot of Fontenay le Château was knighted for bringing cherry trees to France from Asia. Thereafter the family coat of arms depicted a cherry tree. It was also in France that the 'Montmorency' cultivar was first developed. Louis XVI popularized cherries throughout France by encouraging cultivation and experimenting with new varieties. His wife, Marie Antoinette, ordered that cherry trees be planted in the 'hamlet' given to her by Louis, and was even known to have cherries arranged in her elaborate hairstyles.[9]

While cherry cultivation was growing throughout Europe, sweet cherries were imported to India from Kabul during the Mughal emperor Akbar's reign from 1556 to 1605. Akbar's royal gardeners developed even sweeter varieties of cherries.[10]

In the New World, chokecherries had been known to Native Americans for centuries, and seventeenth-century European settlers brought in new varieties of sweet and sour cherries. French settlers from Normandy planted cherry trees in the upper Midwest, near the St Lawrence River and Great Lakes. The tree stock planted by the French eventually gave rise to huge commercial cherry-growing orchards in Michigan and other areas of the upper Midwest, starting in the mid-1800s and continuing to this day. The first commercial

Bartolomeo Bimbi, *Cherries*, 1699, oil on canvas.

sour cherry orchard, Ridgewood Farms, was created in 1893 near Traverse City, Michigan.

In the eighteenth century, George Washington and Thomas Jefferson, both prolific gardeners, grew several varieties of cherries in their extensive gardens. In 1816 Jefferson wrote to a friend that the 'Carnation' cherry is 'so superior to all others that no other deserves the name of cherry'.[11]

Pioneers and fur traders from the eastern United States brought cherry trees west. In 1847 Henderson Lewelling transported three hundred cherry trees from Iowa to Oregon, and by 1875 the cultivation of sweet cherries in the Willamette Valley in Oregon was flourishing.

The English word 'cherry' has ancient roots. In approximately 300 BCE the Greek philosopher Theophrastus described a large tree with red, round fruit that he named *kerasos* in honour of the town Kerasum, which is today the city of Giresun in northern Turkey. It is not clear whether the town received its name because of the cherries grown there, or the other way round.[12]

Postcard of 'Loads of cherries leaving the Morgan orchard,
Traverse City, Michigan', 1933.

The Romans, credited with cultivating cherries throughout
their empire, used the Latin name *cerasum*. From this Latin root word
was derived the Old French *cherise*, the Modern French *cerise*, the
Spanish *cereza*, the Italian *ciliegia* and the Portuguese *cereja*. In early
Anglo-Saxon English the word for cherry was *ciris*, but later Middle
English was influenced by the French plural word for cherry, *cherise*,
and rendered it as *cheri*, subsequently cherry. Some cherry-producing
countries have more specific words for cherry varieties. For example,
in France all cherries are generally called *cerises*, but sweet cherries are
often called *bigarreaux* and sour cherries *griottes*.

Taxonomically speaking, cherry trees belong to the genus *Prunus*,
within the rose family, Rosaceae. The *Prunus* genus includes plums,
peaches, nectarines, apricots, almonds and cherries. The fruits from
this genus, including cherries, are commonly called stone fruits.

Cultivars are plants that have been produced in cultivation by
selective breeding. In contrast to a cultivar, a 'variety' can often be
found growing and reproducing naturally. The objectives of breeding
programmes include manipulating fruit size and firmness, fruit quality, self-fertility, extended harvest season, adaptability to mechanical
harvest, precocity (earlier fruit-bearing), productivity, resistance to

rain-induced cracking, and resistance to diseases and insects. Breeding for rootstock focuses on such traits as vigour, growth habit, precocity and fruit quality, graft compatibility and propagation, pest resistance and adaptability to soil and environmental conditions.

Prunus avium

Prunus avium is commonly called the sweet cherry. (In the British Isles it is also called the wild cherry. Confusingly, however, outside the British Isles the name wild cherry is also used for naturally occurring cherry trees.)

Sweet cherry trees grow to 9–12 metres (30–40 ft) and have a pyramidal shape with branches growing fairly upright. They can live for up to sixty years. Based on fruit colour, shape and texture, sweet cherries can be subdivided into four groups: black geans, amber geans, hearts and bigarreaux.[13] DNA research of plant genotypes will assist in germplasm collection management and the selection of genotypes in cherry-breeding programmes.[14] For example, the UK's National Fruit Collection at Brogdale Farm, Kent, is home to more than three hundred varieties of sweet cherries, which is still only a small subset of the over nine hundred estimated varieties.

The 'Black Tartarian' is one of the oldest cherries under cultivation. At one time the variety was one of the most commonly planted of all sweet cherries. It was mentioned by the English horticulturist John Rea in 1676 but most likely originated many years before that date. Robert Dodonee, a naturalist from Malines, Belgium, probably first mentioned it in 1552. According to William Hooker's book *Pomona Londinensis*, written in 1818, 'Black Tartarian', also known as 'Black Circassian' or 'Ronalds' Large Black Heart', was thought to have been introduced into England from Circassia, Russia, by Hugh Ronalds in 1794. It was subsequently introduced into the United States in the nineteenth century. One of the oldest known grafted cherry trees that is still fruitful is a 'Black Tartarian' planted in Eugene, Oregon, in 1860.[15] Unfortunately, the fruit of the 'Black Tartarian' is not suitable

Cherry espalier at Hampton Court Palace, Surrey, England.

for commercial growing because it does not ship well, is very soft, doesn't hold its shape and is susceptible to brown rot.

Cherry-naming confusion abounds, as illustrated by the story of Henderson Lewelling transporting his three hundred cherry trees in tubs from Iowa to Oregon in 1847. Reportedly, the label of one of the trees was lost and it was renamed 'Royal Ann', but the cultivar was in reality 'Napoleon'; both names persist to this day.[16]

'Bing' is currently the leading commercial sweet cherry variety in the U.S. It is commonly used as a basis of comparison for discussing sweet cherry selections. For example, 'Chelan' is harvested ten to twelve days before 'Bing', and 'Lapins' ten to fourteen days after. 'Bing' cherries are mostly produced for fresh market as they ship well, but they do tend to crack if exposed to rain near harvest time. The 'Bing' cultivar is a cross-bred graft from the 'Black Republican' cherry and was developed in 1875 by Oregon horticulturist Seth Lewelling, who named it after his Chinese foreman, Ah Bing.[17]

'Burlat' is a native French cherry similar to 'Bing' and is the most popular sweet cherry in France, accounting for over 50 per cent of the cherries sold there annually. Leonard Burlat, a soldier returning from the First World War to his home town in France, brought with him cuttings from a wild cherry tree and cultivated them.[18] The 'Burlat' cherry has been designated France's official cherry, having received the *Apellation d'origine contrôlée*, a French government certification that designates a geographical indication.[19]

The sweet cherry variety 'Ferrovia' was named in the 1930s, when the strain was developed from the seed of a tree growing near the

'Black Tartarian' variety in a watercolour by Mary Daisy Arnold, early 20th century.

railway lines northwest of Sammichele di Bari in Italy.[20] It now has the Italian-controlled designation of origin, *Denominazione di origine protetta*.

The sweet cherry variety 'Rainier' was introduced in the twentieth century and was the result of a cross between 'Bing' and 'Van'. This cherry is a creamy yellow colour blushed with pink. Blush cherries require careful handling and packing at harvest, to prevent bruising

Vintage wooden cherry-crate labels from the 1960s.

'Rainier' cherries are a sweet cherry variety often used in canning.

and ugly brown marks. 'Rainier' is susceptible to powdery mildew and rain cracking. This fruit is mostly suitable for brining or fresh consumption.

Most sweet cherry varieties require a pollinator, and breeding programmes search for self-pollinating varieties to overcome this problem. As an example, the self-fertile 'Stella' cultivar was introduced by the Canadian Department of Agriculture Research Station in 1968. Although it does not require a pollinator, it will do better with one. Not only is 'Stella' self-fruiting, it is a good pollinator for 'Bing'. Another popular self-fruitful variety is 'Lapins'. In choosing a variety of pollinator for sweet cherries, it is important to consider the flowering-time-related compatibility of cultivars.

'Mazzard' is a vigorous rootstock from *Prunus avium* and is used for grafting various sweet cherry cultivars. It is commercially important and is often cultivated where there is poor drainage. 'Mazzard' produces a mature tree with a height of 6 metres (20 ft) or more. Although it is relatively slow-growing, 'Mazzard' rootstock is good for traditional orchards. However, the large trees are more difficult to harvest and protect from birds. 'Krymsk 6' is a semi-dwarfing rootstock from Russian breeding programmes that has recently become more available. 'Colt' is a rootstock developed in England in 1958 from a cross between *P. avium* and *P. pseudocerasus*, and is noted for its resistance to virus-caused cherry stem pitting, root rot, bacterial canker and gopher damage.[21]

Prunus cerasus

Prunus cerasus is commonly called the sour, tart or acid cherry. The sour cherry is probably an accidental cross between sweet and ground cherry (*P. fruticosa*). *P. fruticosa* is considered to be a parent of both *P. avium* and *P. cerasus*.

There are two major kinds of tart cherries, morello and Amarelle, and they can be distinguished by their pigmentation. Amarelle cherries have red skins but a whitish flesh, while morello cherries have both red skin and flesh.

While there are over three hundred varieties of sour cherry, cultivation is dominated by just a few of the cultivars. In central Europe the main sour cherry cultivar is called 'Scattenmorelle', or 'English Morello'.[22] Sour cherries were popular in Britain during the time of Henry VIII, and became a common crop for Kentish growers. When English colonists arrived in the U.S., the first sour cherry trees they planted were called 'Kentish Red'.

An Amarelle cherry, the 'Montmorency', dominates sour cherry production in the U.S., accounting for about 90 per cent of the total.[23]

'Cerise de Montmorency' variety in a watercolour by Deborah Passmore, early 20th century.

This four-hundred-year-old cultivar originated in the Montmorency Valley in France.[24]

Concern over the limited genetic diversity in U.S. sour cherry varieties led researchers to investigate several varieties of European sour cherries. In 1996 Michigan State University grew strains of a sour cherry originating in Újfehértó, Hungary, and trademarked the variety 'Balaton'.[25] Compared to 'Montmorency', it is larger, firmer, deeper in colour and has a sweeter, juicy flesh.

Sour cherries have greater tolerance for poor drainage and are more resistant than sweet varieties to damage caused by pests and diseases. They are almost all self-fertile, unlike most sweet cherry varieties. Smaller pollinator populations are needed for these varieties because pollen has to be moved only within individual flowers, rather than from tree to tree.

'Gisela' is a rootstock developed in Germany from a cross between *P. cerasus* and *P. canescens*. It is a popular rootstock in Europe as it tends to have earlier flowering and fruit ripening by two to four days. This potential for earlier ripening offers an advantage for the cultivar because an early harvest provides higher returns. However, this is a disadvantage in frost-susceptible areas.[26] 'Gisela 5' is a semi-dwarfing rootstock that appeals to domestic gardeners because it solves the problem of excessive tree size, growing only 2–3 metres (6–10 ft) tall.

The 'Duke' cherry is a hybrid of *P. avium* and *P. cerasus*.[27] It resembles the sweet cherry in appearance but has a tart flavour inherited from the sour cherry.

Prunus serotina

Prunus serotina goes by several names, including American black cherry, wild black cherry, mountain black cherry and rum cherry. The last probably comes from the fact that the fruit was used to flavour rum or brandy, making a product commonly called 'cherry bounce', a favourite colonial beverage of the eighteenth century. However, *Prunus serotina* is best known for its strong, hard and closed-grained wood, which has a rich, reddish-brown colour. Those qualities make it a valuable wood for cabinet- and furniture making.

Black cherry is the largest of the native cherries and can grow to a height of 24–30 metres (80–100 ft), with a trunk diameter of 1.2–1.5 metres (4–5 ft). Some trees can live as long as 250 years. As a shade-intolerant species, it is usually found in successional vegetation or in forest openings, old fields and along fence rows; anywhere there is adequate sunlight with limited competition from other trees. Because its seeds can remain in the soil a long time and still have the ability to sprout, black cherry often dominates secondary succession growth after logging or fire.

In the U.S., coal mining has disturbed millions of acres of forests. Black cherry trees have often been planted to revegetate these areas and prevent erosion, enhance wildlife habitat and eventually provide future economic returns when the trees are mature enough to be logged.

The black cherry tree is native to North America but was introduced into Europe in the twentieth century as an ornamental plant. It became locally naturalized there and was later planted extensively

Cross-section of a black cherry tree (*Prunus serotina*).

by foresters in many countries. Black cherry is sometimes considered an invasive species in Europe, and Dutch children sometimes perform service field trips to pull out black cherry saplings.[28]

Prunus virginiana

Prunus virginiana is commonly known as chokecherry. Sometimes it is called wild cherry – a name that causes confusion, as the same term is used in the UK for sweet cherries (*Prunus avium*). It is also known as bird cherry, causing confusion with *Prunus padus*, which is also called a bird cherry.

Chokecherry covers a large geographic area in its native North America. Best described as a shrub or small tree, it rarely exceeds 9 metres (30 ft) in height. Many indigenous people used it as a medicinal for such varied conditions as sore throats, diarrhoea and post-partum hemorrhaging, and it was also used as a food. The fruit's

Chokecherry (*Prunus virginiana*) found growing wild along a cultivated cherry orchard in Traverse City, Michigan.

Ancient Japanese *sakura* in bloom, Toji Temple, Kyoto, Japan.

name came from its bitter, astringent taste. Because of this, it is more often used for making jelly than eaten fresh. In 1629 chokecherry was exported from North America to England, where it is primarily considered to be an ornamental landscape plant.

Prunus serrulata

Prunus serrulata is commonly called Japanese cherry, hill cherry, oriental cherry or East Asian cherry. There are hundreds of cultivars

Single-blossom cherry, Ikuta-jinja shrine, Kobe, Japan.

and varieties, such as *P. serrulata* var. *spontanea*, known as the mountain cherry.[29]

    Flourishing in its native countries of Japan, Korea and China as well as in many temperate regions of the world, *Prunus serrulata* is grown primarily as a flowering ornamental tree. While cherry blossoms naturally have five petals, some cultivars have up to a hundred petals per blossom. The petal colours can range from white to pink.

There are also many other species of *Prunus* that are called Japanese flowering cherries. These include *Prunus pendula*, a weeping cherry, and *Prunus incise*, which can be grown as a bonsai.[30]

Another flowering cherry is *Prunus serrulata* var. *speciosa* (Oshima cherry), prized for its blossoms and also its edible leaves, which are used to make a rice cake called *sakuramochi*.

Japanese cherry trees have always been bred for their blossoms, not fruit. Some trees do produce small cherries but these are generally too sour for human consumption, though birds like them. The Japanese government dedicated five historic cherry trees as National

Double-blossom cherry, Ikuta-jinja shrine, Kobe, Japan.

Natural Monuments in 1922. In Fujinomiya, Shizuoka Prefecture, there is the eight-hundred-year-old wild cherry tree, a Yamazakura, named Kariyado no Gebazakura, thought to be the tree to which the first shogun, Minamoto no Yoritomo, tied his horse.[31] Japan's fifteenth Edo shogun, the poet Tokugawa Yoshinobu, likens this connection to the relationship of the Japanese people to the beautiful old tree:

> Alas it not only holds horses but also the beholder's hearts, this wild cherry tree.[32]

Prunus mahaleb

Prunus mahaleb is commonly known as mahaleb cherry, rock cherry or St Lucie cherry. The mahaleb cherry is a deciduous shrub or small tree, reaching 10 metres (32 ft) tall. Because of its dwarf stature and

'Mahaleb Cherry' variety in a watercolour by Royal Charles Steadman, early 20th century.

strong root system, which is not sensitive to many diseases, as well as its frost resistance and tolerance to drought, it is frequently used as the rootstock for other cultivated sweet or sour cherry varieties.

The mahaleb cherry has been grown for centuries in eastern Europe, the Middle East and North Africa, both for its fruits and its almond-tasting seeds inside the stone. The edible fruits are dark red, small and slightly bitter, and a purple dye may be obtained from them. More commonly, however, the soft interior of the seed, the kernel or embryo, is ground and used as a spice called mahaleb. There are many alternative spellings of the Arabic name for this spice: *mahlab*, *mahalab*, *mahleb*, *mahaleb*, *mahlep*, *mahalep*, *mahlepi*, *machlepi* and *makhlepi*. It has the flavour and smell of bitter almonds. An oil may also be obtained from the seeds, which contain a high level of polyunsaturated fatty acids.

Cherry Orchard Management

Cherry trees grow in temperate climatic zones where cooler temperatures provide the chilling requirement for flower induction. Winter temperatures need to be below 7°C (45°F) for about 900–1,000 hours for most sweet cherry varieties, and slightly longer for sour cherries. Cherry seeds require exposure to cold temperature to germinate. For this reason, cherries cannot grow in tropical climates.

Flower development and fruit set is affected by late spring frosts, although sour cherries are hardier and generally bloom later than sweet cherries. Ripening cherries can suffer from too much sun. Rain can cause the sweet cherries to crack (when they absorb extra moisture and split open). Sweet cherries flourish better in regions with dry summer growing conditions because the fruit is susceptible to cracking in regions with more rain. All these factors – temperature, sunlight and rain – need to be balanced to ensure a successful harvest.

Climatic variations such as late spring frosts or low midwinter temperatures can contribute to wide fluctuations in the supply of cherries from year to year. For example, an early May freeze event in

Michigan in 2017 reduced production of tart cherries by 23 per cent compared to the previous year.[33]

Many sweet cherry varieties cannot pollinate their own kind and thus need a compatible pollinator cherry tree planted nearby. With few exceptions ('Stella', 'Lapins' and 'Sweetheart' cultivars), sweet cherries need a pollinator, but not all sweet cherries can act as a pollinator. Sour cherry varieties are self-fertile and will pollinate themselves.

Cherry trees are entomophilous, meaning they are pollinated by insects. The introduction of honeybees (*Apis mellifera*) can increase yield by two to four times if the orchard is large or other wild pollinators are lacking. Because cherries bloom early and honeybees will not forage below 15°C (60°F) or in windy or damp conditions, fruit set and yield may suffer if cherry trees blossom when environmental conditions are not optimum for the bees. Typically, honeybees visit flowers in the morning, so beehives should face south, to warm them in the morning and encourage bee activity. Orchard management practices such as pesticide applications, or mowing that disrupts the bees' morning activity, may significantly impact the success of pollination.

A sour cherry tree usually takes three to five years to produce its first crop, and seven to eleven years to reach full maturity. A sweet

Netting over cherry trees at Tougas Family Farm, Northborough, Massachusetts.

Cherries protected by homemade bird netting on a small farm outside Lviv, Ukraine.

cherry tree typically produces its first crop in five to seven years. Sweet and sour cherry trees may be productive for sixteen to twenty years, although they may live far longer. There may be variations in precociousness, longevity and productivity, depending on the rootstock.

Cherry stones have evolved to be eaten by birds. The stones do not germinate well unless they have been through a bird's crop and digestive system. Also, the birds help disseminate the seeds far away from the parent tree. Planting the seeds of a particular cherry will produce a plant of the same species unless it has been pollinated with pollen from a different species, in which case the seedling will be a hybrid between those species.

Commercial growers and domestic gardeners use grafting as a reliable and cost-effective way to propagate cherry trees. Grafting involves taking a desirable cultivar and selecting a piece of last year's growth with three to four buds. This is called a scion and is attached to the lower part of another, usually young, plant called the rootstock by physically joining the stems of the scion and rootstock. The two plants will grow together if the graft is successful. The scion becomes the upper part of the mature plant and is true to its cultivar.

Grafting preserves the exact properties of known varieties and their cultivars. The rootstock will impart certain predictable qualities to the fruit trees, most notably size, disease resistance, precociousness and coping with a range of environmental conditions. Interesting novel specimens can be developed by grafting several cultivars on one tree.

In addition to sources of aesthetic pleasure, Mughal gardens were also sites for horticultural experiments. Grafting was a technique successfully used in these gardens: the emperor Jahangir 'explicitly ordered officials in Kashmir to graft sweet cherry in the (imperial) gardens, and so make it plentiful'.[34]

Today, gardeners continue to experiment with grafting. Domestic and community gardeners have embarked upon a grassroots movement to preserve the genetic diversity and heirloom varieties of cherries through creative grafting; scions are preserved and shared among these enthusiasts.

Several different cherries are among the forty different varieties of stone fruits that artist Sam Van Aken, a professor at Syracuse University, has grafted to create a stunning work of art, with different-coloured blossoms and producing different fruit all summer. The artist planted the trees of his *Tree of Forty Fruits* in locations where the general public would enjoy his unique living sculptures.[35]

Pliny the Elder (23–79 CE), in the *Natural History*, mentions various methods of grafting trees, but demonstrated a lack of understanding about grafting compatibility:

> This branch of civilized life has long since been brought to the very highest pitch of perfection, for man has left nothing untried here. Hence it is that we find Virgil speaking of grafting the nut-tree on the arbutus, the apple on the plane, and the cherry on the elm.[36]

Planting fruit trees too close to one another leads to competition for light and nutrients. High-density planting may require pruning to allow in more light and permit adequate air circulation. Trees that are regularly pruned are more apt to produce quality fruit.

It is more efficient to train trees early to grow in the desired position, rather than pruning them later. Espalier training, creating a tree structure in two dimensions using trellises or walls, has long been a successful practice. The planting of the King's Kitchen Garden (*Le Potager du Roi*) at Versailles has been carefully recreated in its original location, including a wall with espaliered cherry trees. George Washington, an admirer of French gardens, included espaliered cherry trees in the kitchen garden in his home at Mount Vernon in Virginia. The trees continue to flourish and a cherry jam is produced from them and sold in the shop on the grounds each year. Similar to espaliering, a new tree-training system called Upright Fruiting Offshoots (UFO) is being developed with sweet cherries in order to take advantage of cherry's natural upright growth habit.

Modern cherry orchards are typically planted in high density, using dwarf rootstocks and training systems designed to facilitate maximum sunlight exposure, higher fruit yield and quality, and easier worker access. Successful orchard management includes extending the season with different cultivars, replacing ageing trees, terracing on hillsides, treatments to prevent or control diseases and the use of nets to limit pest and bird damage.

Sour cherries are relatively resistant to diseases, but sweet cherries are highly susceptible. Brown rot, also called blossom blight, is a fungal disease caused by *Monilinia laxa* and *M. fructicola*, but control is relatively simple with one or two fungicide sprays during bloom development. Fruit rot is also caused by the same fungi, and this can cause post-harvest decay. Preventative sprays applied before harvest may help reduce this problem.

Bacterial canker is produced by *Pseudomonas syringae*. Cankers can girdle and kill individual branches and sometimes entire trees, especially young ones. At this time, there are no truly effective controls

Emperor Jahangir (r. 1605–27) overseeing the grafting of cherry trees in a Mughal garden, 17th century.

against them, although copper sprays and antibiotics have been used with some success.

Cherry fruit flies are a common pest in the cherry industry. Eradicating the insect's larva is crucial to a successful crop. Monitoring protocols have been developed so that when the first fly has been detected, there is a limited seven- to ten-day time frame in which to apply the appropriate organophosphate insecticide.[37]

Drosophila suzukii, or spotted-wing drosophila, is a fruit fly native to Asia and was first detected in North America and Europe in 2008–10.[38] As a newly invasive pest, it is currently the subject of extensive research regarding control measures. The female lays eggs within ripening fruit on a plant before harvest. The hatched larvae feed on the fruit, causing it to soften, bruise and wrinkle, opening it up to rot and ruining its marketability. Current research is focusing on resistant cultivars and better timing of treatment.

The Environmental Working Group, based in Washington, DC, featured cherries at number seven on its '2017 Dirty Dozen' list of produce containing pesticide residues.[39] Cherry growers have problems dealing with powdery mildew and black cherry aphid without resorting to pesticides.

Birds play an important part in spreading cherry stones, but they also are the sworn enemy of cherry growers, who go to great lengths

Orchardist James Martin with heritage cherry trees in the Tamar Valley, Devon, UK.

to prevent them quickly demolishing the fruit crop. Birds will eat or damage the fruit, leading to reduced quality and greater susceptibility to pests and pathogens. Under-ripe cherries will not ripen after being picked from the tree, so there is no point picking the cherries before they are ripe in order to foil the birds. In the Tamar Valley in Devon, UK, orchardist James Martin witnessed a flock of starlings destroying an entire year's fruit harvest in a matter of hours. Pigeons are also a problem, as they typically pick at the fruit just before it's ripe. The only effective way to protect the cherry crop from birds is to net the trees, or at least individual branches. Decoys, hanging CDs, silver foil and other solutions don't frighten birds away for long enough.

While not practical advice for a commercial orchard, a home gardener can reflect on the words of the English politician and writer Joseph Addison (1672–1719), 'I value my garden more for being full of blackbirds than of cherries, and very frankly give them fruit for their songs.'[40]

Cherry Production and Consumption

Everyone likes cherries, but consumption is highest in the former Soviet Union and eastern bloc countries. If you assume cherries are consumed mainly in the country of their production, cherry consumption ranges from about 1.5 kilograms (3 lb) per person in the U.S. to 6 kilograms (13 lb) per person in Hungary.[41]

According to data from the Food and Agriculture Organization (FAO) of the United Nations, in 2016 Russia was the world's largest cherry importer, accounting for roughly 15 per cent of world imports, followed by Austria and Germany with 12 per cent each, although the Austrian consumption per capita is ten times larger than Germany's. The UK ranked fourth, with 8 per cent. In the UK the demand for cherries far exceeds domestic production, and local commercial orchards were able to supply only about 5 per cent of demand in 2009. However, cherry production is increasing in the UK, aided particularly by advanced covering technology and new varieties of dwarfing

Top 10 Cherry-producing Countries by Metric Tonnes Per Annum		
1	Turkey	445,556
2	USA	329,852
3	Iran	172,000
4	Spain	118,220
5	Italy	110,766
6	Chile	83,903
7	Romania	82,808
8	Uzbekistan	80,000
9	Russian Federation	77,000
10	Greece	73,380

rootstocks, which increase the yield and extend the traditionally short growing season in the UK.

Cherries are considered a high-value crop. Global sales from sweet cherry exports by country amounted to U.S.$2.4 billion in 2016. The chart given here, using 2016 FAOSTAT data, shows the top ten cherry-producing countries by metric tonnes.[42]

Data from FAOSTAT in 2016 for sweet and sour cherries combined indicate that Turkey is the number one cherry producer at 21.5 per cent of world production. The U.S. is number two, accounting for 13.1 per cent; until the last decade, it was the number one producer.

Chile is the sixth largest cherry producer and the second largest exporter, after the U.S. Chile previously focused on exporting to the U.S. and EU markets, but Hong Kong and China have since become the largest importers of Chilean cherries. They help account for Chile's remarkable 807 per cent growth in cherry exports between 1995 and 2010. This growth is a result of improvements in the shipping of cherries over the long distance from Chile to China, and marketing efforts capitalizing on Chilean cherries ripening at the same time as the Chinese New Year.

The Health Benefits of Cherries

While people today generally aren't hesitant about eating fresh cherries, there was a time when many fresh fruits were considered unhealthy by medical authorities.[43] The second-century physician Galen cautioned against eating fruits, believing them at best to be a laxative. He wrote, 'We never need them for food, but only as a medication.'[44]

In medieval theory, all foods were considered 'medicine', as food was perceived to keep the body healthy. The *Tacuinum Sanitatis* is a well-illustrated fifteenth-century health handbook based on the *Taqwīm assiḥḥah* (Maintenance of Health), an eleventh-century Arab medical treatise by Ibn Butlan of Baghdad. *Tacuinum* discusses the beneficial or harmful properties of foods and plants. The hundreds of illustrations provide invaluable details of daily life at the time, including cooking and agricultural activities. Cherry harvests are illustrated and readers are told the health benefits and uses for the fruit. Sweet cherries are thought to 'loosen the stomach'. Sour cherries reportedly cure bilious attacks and dry out and settle upset stomachs.[45]

Chinese herbalists view cherries' characteristics as warm (Yang), meaning they have a warming effect on the body, and sweet, meaning they have properties that slow down acute reactions and neutralize the toxic effects of other foods as well as lubricating and nourishing the body.

Texts from the Salerno School, a late medieval school in Salerno, Italy, said of cherries:

Cherry, good fruit, what blessings you procure!
Sweet to the taste, you make our humours pure
Sending new blood to run through every vein,
Relieving gallstone sufferers of their pain.[46]

The historical use of cherries as a diuretic to lower blood pressure makes sense because we now know that cherries have a high potassium

Trade card for Ayer's
Cherry Pectoral,
19th century.

content. The current recommended daily requirement for potassium
is 3.5 grams. One can get 10 per cent of this requirement from one
cup (154 g) of cherries.

Cherries are considered healthy due to their content of minerals
(potassium, calcium, iron, magnesium) and vitamins (A, C, B6, E and
folic acid). Boron present in cherries aids bone health. Cherries contain virtually no fat or sodium.

Numerous articles and reports over the last decade refer to cherries as a 'superfood'. The *Daily Mail* on 26 September 2008 headlined

the benefits of consuming them in liquid form: 'Cherry Juice Hailed as Superfood with Equivalent of 23 Portions of Fruit in a Single Glass'. The bright colour of cherries, due to natural colourants called anthrocyanins, is not only attractive but adds to their perceived nutritional value. These colourants, belonging to a group of compounds called flavonoids, also possess antioxidant properties.

Antioxidants fight free radicals, and thereby reduce the risk of cancer, slow signs of ageing, ward off heart disease, lower the risk of stroke, and reduce inflammation and the risk of gout. Antioxidant potency levels are measured by the Oxygen Radical Absorbance Capacity (ORAC). The ORAC value of fresh tart cherries is one and a half times greater than that of an equal amount of fresh strawberries.[47]

Cherries are one of the few known edible sources of melatonin, an antioxidant produced naturally by the body that helps regulate biorhythm and natural sleep patterns. Some researchers concluded that consumption of tart cherry juice concentrate improves sleep duration and quality.[48]

Of course, there is no such thing as the perfect food, and some people are allergic to cherries. Eating them could cause mouth tingling, and swelling of the lips, tongue, roof of the mouth, and throat. They can also cause nausea and vomiting, hives, nasal congestion, a metallic taste and, rarely, anaphylaxis. Allergies to cherries are not that common; cherries are not in the top eight on the list of allergens. Individuals allergic to cherries are usually also allergic to other stone fruits such as peaches, apricots and plums.[49]

The cherry bark, twigs, wilted leaves and pits contain a cyanogenetic glucoside called amygdalin. Hydrolysis of glycosides results in the release of hydrogen cyanide. The potential for this to cause harm to humans and animals will be discussed in Chapter Four.

Referring to fruit in general, researchers have discovered that the more of it you eat, the happier you will be. A 2016 *Psychology Today* article reviewing this research is aptly titled 'Happiness Is (Literally) a Bowl of Cherries'.[50]

two

Blossoms: Aesthetics of the Ephemeral
6✿9

Would you powder the blossoms of a cherry tree?

MARIE ANTOINETTE'S DIARY[1]

Marie Antoinette asks this question in her 11 March 1769 diary entry, referring to the stunning natural beauty of the blossoms on cherry trees she had requested for her private 'hamlet' given to her by King Louis XVI. Cherry blossoms hardly require embellishment; no need to gild a lily.

Defining characteristics of the many ornamental cherry varieties include the number of petals, the colour of the blossoms (white to pink, even some yellow and green), their fragrance, the blooming season, the appearance of the leaves and the overall shape of the tree. Cherry blossoms can have between five and three hundred petals and may be divided into four categories, based on the number of petals: single, semi-double, double or chrysanthemum.

While flowering cherry trees had been cultivated in Japan for centuries and horticultural practices there were quite advanced, until the 1850s the flora of Japan were little known beyond the islands themselves. Based specifically on their aesthetic preferences, the Japanese had selected variants of ornamental cultivars of cherry trees from the wild for their gardens as early as 794 CE.[2] Eighteenth-century residents of Tokyo and Kyoto already enjoyed the spectacular beauty of avenues lined with flowering cherry trees. Garden historian Christopher Thacker wrote that the Japanese

Several varieties of Japanese cherries grafted onto a single cherry tree,
Ikuta-jinja shrine, Kobe, Japan.

garden was already 'infinitely sophisticated while we in the west
were still in bearskins'.[3]

According to the Flower Association of Japan, there are over 290
species, varieties and hybrids of Japanese flowering cherries. Two of
the most well-known and cherished varieties are the pink
'Kwazuzakura', the earliest blossoming in Japan, and 'Somei Yoshino'
with flowers that are almost pure white, with a hint of very light pink
colouring near the stem. The colour of the blossoms may change
from bud to bloom. In her book *'Cherry' Ingram: The Englishman Who*

Saved Japan's Blossoms, Naoko Abe documented the preference of Japanese governments for planting 'Somei Yoshino' cherry trees, to the exclusion of all other varieties in nineteenth- and twentieth-century Japan, as a symbol for Japan's then expansionist ambitions.[4] Collingwood Ingram, nicknamed 'Cherry', championed the diversity of varieties, particularly what appeared in the early 1900s to be the disappearing *Prunus taihaku*, 'Great White Cherry'.[5]

Today the ornamental cherry is widely dispersed in USDA plant hardiness zones 5–8. These temperate zones of the Northern Hemisphere include Japan, China, Korea, Europe, West Siberia, India, Canada and the United States. Because of the cultural importance of cherry blossoms in Japan, a detailed history exists of the timing of their blooms, both in records dating from the eighth century BCE and in more recent documents from the USDA. For more than fifty years Thomas Jefferson kept detailed notes of the blossoming dates of the cherry trees on his Virginia plantation, Monticello, as he experimented with varieties of plants from all over the world. The records show that he planted cherry trees along the area he called the 'long, grass walk' to provide shade. His data indicate that cherry trees are now blossoming earlier as a result of climate change.[6]

In his 1625 essay *Of Gardens*, Francis Bacon notes:

> I do hold it, in the royal ordering of gardens, there ought to be gardens, for all the months in the year; in which severally things of beauty may be then in season . . . In April . . . the cherry tree in blossom . . . There is a cherry-tree that hath double blossoms; but that tree beareth no fruit.[7]

In Britain Algernon Freeman-Mitford (1837–1916), who in the 1860s had travelled widely in Japan as second secretary to the British legation, imported flowering cherry trees. In his garden at Batsford in Gloucestershire he planted an array of different cherry trees, which eventually provided the foundation of the National Collection of Japanese Flowering Cherries, today boasting more than 115 varieties.[8]

Why do cherry blossoms attract such attention, rather than, say, the plum, pear or peach? The answer lies in the unique qualities of the cherry tree when it is in flower: the brief bloom period (the peak lasts only two or three days) and the exuberance and density of the blossoms. Blossoming cherry trees are celebrated wherever they thrive, but credit goes first to the Japanese for attributing deep cultural meaning to cherry blossoms. The manner in which the Japanese revere cherry blossoms (*sakura*) borders on worship. In ancient Japan cherry blossoms assumed great importance because they announced the rice-planting season and were used to predict the year's rice harvest. Their fleeting beauty was celebrated as a metaphor for the ephemeral nature of life, and they were praised in numerous poems as early as the Heian era (794–1185 CE). The Japanese made rice wine offerings to the spirits they believed lived in the *sakura* trees.

Author Emiko Ohnuki-Tierney documents the use of cherry blossoms in the Shinto religion and early mythology of Japan as a metaphor for 'life-sustaining energy'.[9] A traditional Japanese spell involves tying a strand of one's hair to a cherry tree as it blossoms, to attract love.

Shinto, which translates as 'Way of the Gods', is the traditional Japanese indigenous animistic belief system. The Shinto scholar and poet Motoori Norinaga (1730–1801) defined the term *mono no aware*, 'the pathos of things', as an underlying current in Japanese culture. He wrote:

> If someone asks
> about the spirit of a true Japanese,
> point to the wild cherry blossom
> shining in the sun.[10]

In Shinto mythology *Konohana-sakura Hime* (Cherry Tree Blossom Blooming Princess) is one of the enshrined deities at the Asama Jinja at Mount Fuji. She married Ninigi, the grandson of the supreme Shinto deity Amaterasu, the sun goddess.[11] She became pregnant and miraculously produced three children in a single night, during which her home was destroyed by a raging fire. Having survived this ordeal, Konohana-sakura Hime is known as the Shinto *kami* who protects mothers during childbirth. In some versions of the story, she was killed in the fire, her life then compared to the ephemeral beauty of the fragile cherry blossom. The goddess of Mount Fuji and all volcanoes, Konohana's symbol is the *sakura*.

The Shinto shrine Hirano Jinja in Kyoto is famed for its cherry blossom connection. Its precincts are home to four hundred cherry trees of fifty different types, which bloom in succession over the course of three or four weeks in spring. The shrine is especially known for its beauty at night. An annual cherry blossom festival has been held there since the reign of Emperor Kazan in 985 CE; it is now celebrated on 10 April every year.[12]

Hundreds of trees in Japan are thought to be inhabited by spirits called *kodama*, many of which inhabit flowering cherry trees. These trees are said to bloom on particular anniversaries. A famous cherry tree myth, 'The Tale of the Milk Nurse Cherry Tree', was introduced to the West by Greek-Irish writer Lafcadio Hearn. The story relates the miraculous blooming of a cherry tree on the anniversary of the death of a devoted wet nurse who unselfishly gives her own life to save that of a child in her care.

A popular Japanese story from a series known as '36 Ghosts' tells of Kurozome, a Japanese cherry tree spirit. Lord Kuronushi, setting out on a quest to overthrow the emperor, interrupts his journey to build a shrine that will ensure his success. He boasts about his plan to use an ancient cherry tree for the wood, but as he is about to cut it down, the spirit appears to him in the form of Kurozume, a legless courtesan with magical powers. Before he can raise his axe, the spirit changes into a cherry branch and thumps the villain thoroughly.[13]

In his article 'What's the Cultural Significance of Cherry Blossoms?' Joseph Castro notes that 'In Buddhism, cherry blossoms also symbolize the transience of life.'[14] The Japanese ornamental cherry tree is known for its short but impressive blooming season, which symbolically describes human life. The Japanese equate the short life of a cherry blossom before it is scattered by the wind and rain with the cycle of human life; it is a reminder to live in the present moment before life fades away and to recognize the importance of the Buddhist concept of non-attachment. Buddhists consider the opening of a cherry blossom a symbol of wisdom because it resembles

Tsukioka Yoshitoshi, *The Spirit of the Komachi Cherry Tree*, 1889, woodblock print.

the mind opening up into a state of enlightenment, mirroring the characteristics of the lotus metaphor so important in Buddhist iconography.

In Japan children were once thought of as mysterious beings in a transitional space between the realm of humans and gods. The gods spoke through them.[15] Part of a long-abandoned, dark Buddhist tradition, *chigo* were beautiful young boys, also known as 'cherry blossoms', chosen to perform certain duties in a Buddhist temple, including serving as sexual partners to older monks, who were forbidden to have sexual relationships with women. Today, the term *chigo*, or 'divine children', refers to young boys who participate in dancing and festival parades. The young boy chosen as a *chigo* for the annual month-long Gion Matsuri in Kyoto, one of the most well-known and popular festivals in Japan, continues to perform the ritual duty of cutting the *shimenawa*, or sacred rope, which begins the parade.[16]

Marking historic events with cherry blossoms has a long history in Japan. Emperor Keitai, the 26th Emperor, planted the Usuzumi cherry tree 1,500 years ago to commemorate his rise to the throne. The Usuzumi tree was declared a National Treasure of Japan in 1922.[17] While the cherry blossom celebrates the fleeting beauty of life, the Japanese equally venerate old age and wisdom by honouring the *Sandaizakura*, the Three Great Cherry Trees thought to be more than 1,000 years old, which are visited by thousands of Japanese during their blooming season.

According to anthropologist Emiko Ohnuki-Tierney, the cherry blossom has been important historically in the development of Japanese nationalism and militarism. The Sakurakai, or Cherry Blossom Society, was an ultra-nationalist secret society established by young officers within the Imperial Japanese Army in September 1930. Its mission was to reorganize the Japanese state along totalitarian militaristic lines, through violent means if necessary. This Shōwa Restoration would reinstate Emperor Hirohito to his former powers in a new military dictatorship, free of party politics and evil bureaucrats.[18]

During the Second World War, cherry blossoms assumed a similar meaning for the Japanese when the five-petalled flowers were painted on the sides of kamikaze warplanes. They were intended to symbolize the brevity and impermanence of life, a metaphor promoted widely by the military in statements such as 'Thou shall die like beautiful falling cherry petals for the emperor.'[19] In addition, cherry blossom motifs appear frequently in Japanese military insignia.

At the Yasukuni Shrine, a monument to soldiers killed while serving their country, established in 1869, cherry blossom trees were planted to console the souls of soldiers. Japanese government propaganda encouraged the people to believe that cherry blossoms were the

Yōshu Chikanobu, 'Cherry Blossom Viewing', from the series *Chiyoda Castle*, 1895, woodblock print.

reincarnation of soldiers killed in battle. Ironically, after the Second World War, cherry trees came to be seen as symbols of peace.

Hanami, the tradition of blossom viewing, is an ancient custom originally adopted from neighbouring China, marking the miraculous reawakening of nature after the long sleep of winter and the first flowering of spring. Though the Chinese preferred the earlier-blooming plum blossom, in Japan *hanami* has long been associated predominately with cherry blossoms. This Japanese preference for cherry is due to the exuberance and vitality of its blossoms and the stunning visual

Japanese *Ohka* (cherry blossom) kamakaze plane decorated with stylized blossom, 1940s.

display they provide in such a very short time. The beautiful massed blossoms resemble clouds, and fallen blossoms are like snowfall. The cherry blossom motif is particularly popular in painting and textile arts and is often combined with running water and waterfalls.[20] It has become common practice annually for everyone from families to office colleagues to head off with snacks and drinks to their favourite temples, parks and river banks to enjoy *hanami*.

The first time the term *hanami* was used synonymously with cherry blossom viewing was in the novel *The Tale of Genji*, written by lady-in-waiting Murasaki Shikibu and published in the year 1008.[21] In the story Prince Genji uses the cherry blossom as a symbol for life forces: youth, love, gaiety, courtship, elegance and the rejuvenation of spring.

As early as the beginning of the Heian period, 794 CE, members of the imperial court regularly celebrated spring by gathering in the carefully cultivated imperial gardens beneath the blossoming cherry trees.[22] The original practice of *hanami* was to brave the cold in order to admire these winter-flowering trees, while drinking warm sake (rice wine) or amazake (a sweeter, low-alcohol or non-alcoholic version) and composing poems to hang on the branches of a cherry tree.[23]

Today poetry about the viewing of cherry blossoms thrives outside of Japan and is popular in Japanese poetry clubs around the world. There are thousands of Japanese poems on the subject, particularly the very short form known as haiku. A recent collection from an International Cherry Blossom Haiku Contest included entries from 101 authors from 27 countries. According to Robert Gill, author of *Cherry Blossom Epiphany*, which contains more than 3,000 Japanese haiku about cherry blossoms, hundreds of thousands of haiku have been written by Japanese poets on this theme. One of the most famous and cherished Japanese poets, Matsuo Bashō (1644–1694),

Scene from the *Tale of Genji*, late 17th century, screen painting.

a student of Zen Buddhism, is credited with developing the short-hand or 'telegram-like' way of writing, as well as *haikai no renga*, a form of collaborative poetry composition. He wrote:

> How many, many things
> They call to mind
> These Cherry Blossoms[24]

Hanami wasn't only for the aristocracy. In his *Tsurezuregusa* (Essays in Idleness), the fourteenth-century priest and author Yoshida Kenko lamented:

> rustic boors . . . take all pleasure grossly. They squirm their way through the crowd to get under the trees; they stare at the blossoms with eyes for nothing else; they drink sake and compose linked verse; and finally they breathlessly break off great branches and cart them away.[25]

This description closely matches the complaints about some of the more raucous *hanami* celebrations in Japan today.

Hanami gradually filtered down through the samurai classes to become a tradition beloved by all echelons of society. In fact, flowering cherries are not a feature of a traditional Japanese garden but are more often planted in parks, where *hanami* is often celebrated as an alcohol-fuelled picnic. During the height of the blossom period, businesses are known to require their office interns to head out first thing in the morning to commandeer a good viewing spot under the cherry trees for the festivities.

Hanami heralds the start of spring. The Japanese reveal their keen observance of the nuances of spring through the variety of terms used for different *hanami* experiences. *Hana-zukare* refers to a sense of fatigue (*tsukare*) caused by overstimulation at the sight of cherry blossoms in

Yozakura 'night sakura' *hanami* in Fukuoka, Japan, 2018.

full bloom, or to the fatigue of dealing with *hanami* crowds. There are usually many weather changes during cherry blossom season. Each has its own term. *Sakura-ame/hana-no-ame* is the lamentable rain (*ame*) that falls around the *hanami* period. *Hana-gumori* refers to cloudy (*kumori*) skies when cherry blossoms bloom. *Hana no Kaze* is the regrettable wind (*kaze*) that sends cherry blossoms scattering, and *hana-bie* is the sudden and temporary cold (*bie*) spell that arrives after the weather has already warmed up during the cherry blossom season.

These viewing parties became a favourite subject for Japanese artists of the Edo period in the form of ukiyo-e woodblock prints, which were widely distributed to the growing merchant class. The term *ukiyo-e* means the Floating World, and refers to the entertainment area of Edo (present-day Tokyo). Woodblock prints by artists of the Edo period, from Hiroshige to Utamaro, often depict cherry blossoms and beautiful geisha.[26] In the visual arts, cherry blossoms are symbolically connected with the motif of the cloud, and many textiles depict cherry blossoms in streams.

Besides announcing spring and new beginnings, cherry blossoms appear in April, which is the start of the school and government years in Japan. Past and present traditions that are part of the cycle of the year, like the *Hinamatsuri* (Girls' Day) festival, observed on 3 March, make reference to cherry blossoms. Tiny vases of cherry blossoms are always placed on a stepped display as part of the *Hinamatsuri* doll arrangements that are part of this celebration, during which parents celebrate their daughters' happiness, growth and good health.

Hanafuda, or *Hanakaruta*, meaning 'flower cards', is a popular Japanese gambling card game played with a deck of 48 cards, consisting of twelve suits representing the months of the year. Each month is represented by a flower, with March represented by the *sakura* blossom. A variety of games are played with these cards, including a version of *Hanafuda* in Hawaii, called Sakura, that uses cards specifically designed with numerical values.[27]

A favourite *hanami* game, Karuta, was popular as long ago as the Heian period, when this lively matching game was played in

Young Japanese girls in *sakura* kimonos, Kyoto, Japan.

competitions at the imperial court. A player has to match the poet card with the card containing the first line of one of that poet's works, many of which have cherry blossom themes. Winning requires lightning speed and dexterity as well as skill in memorizing hundreds of ancient Japanese poems.[28] Today there are many cherry blossom toys and games, including action figures, dolls and even Lego cherry blossom garden sets.

Cherry blossoms play many roles in Japanese culture, from everyday games and celebrations to marking momentous historical events. On 11 March 2011 a massive earthquake (registering a magnitude of 9.0) and accompanying tsunami struck eastern Japan. The earthquake was the fourth strongest ever recorded, and along with the tsunami it claimed more than 15,000 lives, the costliest catastrophe to hit Japan since the Second World War. To commemorate those who suffered this natural disaster, Japanese volunteers have planted trees

Cherry blossom queen in Washington, DC, 1939.

in a uniquely Japanese way. Seventeen thousand pink-flowering cherry trees were planted along the high-water mark of the tsunami unleashed by the earthquake, which at some points reached 10–19 kilometres (6–12 mi.) inland. This living memorial stretches for 169 kilometres (105 mi.). One of its practical objectives is to help local inhabitants know how far inland they need to evacuate to be reasonably safe from any future tsunami.[29]

The Tsunami and the Cherry Blossom is a 2011 documentary film directed by Lucy Walker that describes the preparations made by the earthquake and tsunami survivors for the first cherry blossom season after the disaster, and all the meaning this symbolic period of time has come to signify.[30]

As evidence of how deeply the disaster affected the Japanese people, *hanami* became controversial. Signs posted in Tokyo's Ueno Park by municipal officials in the spring of 2011 suggested that 'people should be mourning the victims of the recent earthquake and tsunami,

not celebrating the coming spring', although many continued the celebration in a more subdued way as a gesture of hope for the future.[31]

Beyond providing a beautiful viewing experience and powerful
symbol of hope, the blossoming ornamental cherry functions as a significant cultural property gifted by the Japanese to friends and allies
as an act of diplomacy and symbol of friendship. Among the recipi-
ents are Canada, Australia, the Netherlands, Germany, Turkey and
the UK. The U.S. programme, Sister Cities International (SCI), began
in 1956 when President Dwight D. Eisenhower proposed a people-
to-people, citizen diplomacy initiative. SCI is a non-profit network
that creates and strengthens partnerships between communities in
the U.S. and other countries. Japan has established more than four
hundred Sister Cities in the U.S., many of which have received gifts
of ornamental cherry trees.

Perhaps the greatest example of a gift of stunningly beautiful
blossoming cherry trees, and the goodwill and pure aesthetic pleasure
generated thereby, is the 1912 gift from Japan of several thousand
ornamental cherry trees to the United States. These trees, which
are planted in the Tidal Basin in Washington, DC, have become an
iconic symbol of the U.S. capital and, as was intended, an impressive
visual reminder of the close historical and political connections and
enduring friendship between the United States and Japan.

One of the heroines of this inspiring story is Mrs Eliza Ruhamah
Scidmore, an adventurous travel-journalist who contributed to the
newly formed National Geographic Society as a writer, editor, photographer and lecturer. She was the first woman to serve as a member of
the Board of Managers and had an iceberg named after her in Glacier
Bay, Alaska. In 1885, after returning to Washington from her first
visit to Japan, where her brother was a diplomat, Scidmore contacted
the U.S. Army superintendent of the Office of Public Buildings and
Grounds with the proposal that cherry trees be planted in mass along
the barren reclaimed Potomac waterfront. Receiving no reply, she
continued to approach every new superintendent, without success,
for the next 24 years. She noted that 'The blooming cherry tree is the

most ideally, wonderfully beautiful tree that nature has to show, and its short-lived glory makes the enjoyment the keener and more poignant.'[32]

During this period, David Fairchild, who was employed by the USDA in the Foreign Seed and Plant Introduction Section, was tasked with finding exotic plants and crops that might be of economic value to the U.S. Fairchild travelled to Japan in 1898 and was impressed by the beauty of the cherry blossoms he observed. He brought back about a hundred cherry trees, which he planted in his backyard in Chevy Chase, Maryland. Joining forces with First Lady Helen Taft, Fairchild formally requested additional trees from the Japanese, and the mayor of Tokyo agreed to provide them.

Unfortunately, the first batch of 2,000 trees arrived diseased and insect-infested in 1910 and had to be burned. But cooperation between the governmental agencies of the two countries, and coordination between Fairchild, Scidmore and the First Lady, resulted in an additional 3,000 new trees arriving in Washington in 1912. Helen Taft and Viscountess Chinda, wife of the Japanese ambassador, presided over a ceremony on 27 March 1912, during which they planted the first two trees from Japan on the north bank of the Tidal Basin in West Potomac Park.

While most cherry blossom trees live for only forty to fifty years, two of the original cherry blossom trees that were planted on that day have survived. These veteran trees are designated with a commemorative plaque placed near the John Paul Jones statue at the south end of 17th Street. In 1981 the United States returned the favour of the original gifted trees when Japanese horticulturists were presented with cuttings from those original trees to replace some cherry trees in Japan that had been destroyed in a devastating flood.

The first Cherry Blossom Festival was held in Washington, DC, in 1935. The festival has grown in popularity and now attracts over 1.5 million people annually, contributing considerably to the local economy. Organizers call the festival 'the nation's greatest springtime celebration'.[33]

Trees can be 'political' in many ways. The 'Cherry Tree Rebellion' took place in 1937 in Washington, DC, where cherry blossoms were already a tourist attraction. Fuelled by deep-seated grievances over lack of self-government for Washington, DC, local citizens protested the removal of trees for the construction of monuments.[34]

In 1941 four cherry trees were cut down in what was thought to be retaliation for the Japanese attack on Pearl Harbor. During the years of the Second World War the cherry trees in Washington, DC, were referred to as 'Oriental' flowering cherries, a designation which undoubtedly contributed to their maintenance and survival.

Roland Maurice Jefferson was the first African American botanist and plant explorer to work at the U.S. National Arboretum, and he was known throughout his career (1957–87) for his work with cherry trees. Jefferson's work, *The Japanese Flowering Cherry Trees of Washington, DC: A Living Symbol of Friendship*, was published in 1977. He later went on to take cuttings from the surviving original 1912 Japanese cherries and had them propagated at the U.S. National Arboretum.[35] It was from these specimens that First Lady Nancy Reagan presented the President Reagan Cherry Tree to the Japanese ambassador in 1981.

In 2012, on the hundredth anniversary of the original gift from Japan, President Barack Obama and Prime Minister Yoshihiko Noda announced several cooperative initiatives, including Friendship Blossoms, with the stated aim of 'strengthening and expanding the United States–Japan relationship in the areas of security cooperation, economic partnership, and cultural people-to-people exchanges'.[36]

For sheer numbers, however, the designation 'Cherry Blossom Capital of the World' goes to Macon, Georgia, which has more than 350,000 trees in bloom every year. What started as a hobby in the 1970s for William Fickling, an amateur horticulturalist, grew to be identified with the city of Macon. An annual cherry blossom festival has been held there since 1982.[37]

The Japanese car company Subaru sponsors an annual cherry blossom festival in Philadelphia in the name of generosity and friendship. Clearly, cherry blossoms have significant market value, which could be called 'flower power', as cherry blossom festivals and celebrations have led to tourism and sponsorship opportunities for businesses globally.

Beginning in 2016, the 'garden city' state of Singapore, having invested considerable resources in the challenging task of making cherry trees bloom in an equatorial tropical climate, has produced a stunning annual cherry blossom festival called 'Blossom Bliss'. Magnificently staged in the flower dome of the public gardens by the bay, there are plans to make this popular and economically successful display an annual event. According to organizers, 'This will be the first time in the world that 23 different varieties of *sakura* come together to bloom in one place.'[38]

In countries where there has also historically been a tradition of growing cherries as a fruit crop, and where cherry harvest festivals are a part of the agricultural cycle, cherry blossom festivals have also become important tourist attractions. In Fundão, Portugal, the blossoms are celebrated as a 'cherry route', and a 'cherry train' transports visitors through the beautiful terraced orchards to view the blossoms.

Hanami flower-viewing in Philadelphia, 2018.

Cherry blossoms in China symbolize love and are linked with female beauty, sexuality and authority, and a woman's power to command her male counterparts through these attributes. Yuyuantan Park is a favourite location for viewing cherry blossoms in Beijing, 'where about 200 of the more than 2,000 cherry trees in the park were given to China by Japan in the early 1970s when the two countries re-established diplomatic ties'.[39]

Modelled somewhat after their Persian ancestors' palace gardens, Islamic gardens typically feature blooming fruit trees, including prized varieties of cherry trees. In her book *Paradise as a Garden in Persia and Mughal India*, Elizabeth B. Moynihan notes, 'According to Jahangir, cherry and apricot trees were successfully brought to Kashmir from Kabul by Akbar.'[40] Both hospitality and gift-giving are important values in Islam. Hospitality is a triangle that links God, the guest and the host.[41]

The act of gift-giving is an important element of behaviour that is used to measure and strengthen relationships between the giver and the recipient. Opulent gardens were frequently the location for occasions of hospitality and were themselves 'gifts' from and to members of the ruling class. D. Fairchild Ruggles writes in *Islamic Gardens and Landscapes*:

> The palace garden was primarily an environmental, economic, and political construct . . . [that] portrays an attitude towards the environment shared by the entire Islamic world, i.e., the taming and glorification of nature enclosed within four walls, juxtaposed with the hostile wild of the outside world.[42]

The garden became a symbol for the omnipotence of the Islamic ruler and a demonstration of his ability to control forces of nature and bestow nature's beauty on whomever he chose. The Shalimar Gardens in Lahore, Pakistan, were laid out by the Mughal emperor Jahangir as a gift for his queen, Nur Jehan.[43]

Cultivating beautiful flowering trees, including cherry trees, for their aesthetic value is a luxury hobby, and sharing this experience with guests is both powerful and generous. In this tradition many private Islamic gardens and their blossoming trees, such as those in Granada, Spain, or in various palaces of Rajasthan in India, have been 'gifted' to the public.

In present-day war-torn Kabul, Afghanistan, the Aga Khan Trust for Culture has recently restored the magnificent Gardens of Babur (Bagh-e Babur) based on the original plantings, which included rows of blossoming cherry trees. This garden is of particular importance as it is one of the earliest surviving Mughal gardens and was created by avid gardener and founder of the Mughal Dynasty Ziihir ad-Din Muhammad Biibur (1483–1530) after his conquest of Kabul in 1504. As the location of his burial tomb, the Bagh-e Babur was a place of pilgrimage for his heirs, Jahangir and Shah Jahan, who commissioned the Taj Mahal. The garden is now open to all and the site is on the list to become a UNESCO World Heritage Site.

George Washington and Thomas Jefferson were described as two of America's 'Founding Gardeners' by author Andrea Wulf in her book by that name.[44] Both men strategically planted cherry trees in their private gardens for ornamental value as well as for fruit-bearing. They modelled the ideas of the *ferme ornée* (ornamental farm) from gardens they observed in England in the early 1800s. Stephen Switzer, in *The Nobleman, Gentleman and Gardener's Recreation* (1715), describes the practice of the *ferme ornée*:

> By mixing the useful and profitable parts of Gard'ning with the Pleasurable in the Interior Parts of my Designs and Paddocks, obscure enclosures, etc. in the outward, My Designs are thereby vastly enlarg'd and both Profit and Pleasure may be agreeably mix'd together.[45]

While George Washington's carefully planned and maintained gardens provided food for the entire plantation community, including the large number of slaves, he also designed them to be beautiful. Records show that eighteenth-century guests visiting Mount Vernon were delighted by the impressive and carefully curated variety of fresh produce, and wrote of enjoying after-dinner walks among the flowering plants and trees, including the blossoming cherry trees.[46]

Today the fruit trees at Mount Vernon continue to be planted in the exact design that Washington documented in his diaries. Records of the plantation show that a large quantity of fruit was needed to make meals, preserves and cider. Details of Washington's interest specifically in cherry trees were recorded in one of the earliest horticultural entries in his diary, dated 24 March 1762, noting receipt of cherry trees from his neighbour and fellow plant enthusiast Colonel George Mason of nearby Gunston Hall.[47]

In 1785 Washington added a fruit garden and orchards to his farms. Meticulous records show that cherries as well as apples, pears, peaches and apricots were among the varieties of fruit trees grown at Mount Vernon. Cherry trees were among those grafted and trained as espaliers, a method of training trees to grow on trellises or on brick walls, literally 'nailed to the wall' by his gardeners.[48] Records show that a visitor to Mount Vernon in 1782 observed, 'There is an immense, extremely well-cultivated garden behind the right wing. The choicest fruits in the country are to be found there.'[49]

In 1783 Louis XVI of France gifted his wife Marie Antoinette with personal gardens at Versailles, including the Queen's Hamlet, which she directed to be planted with blossoming cherry trees, among others. In *From Marie Antoinette's Garden: An Eighteenth-century Horticultural Album*, Élisabeth de Feydeau writes:

> Plants, flowers, and trees were Marie Antoinette's passion and beyond that, her symbolic expression of freedom. At the Petit Trianon, her private kingdom, presented by Louis XVI to his queen like a bouquet of flowers; she found a home of her own and a place where the oppressive shackles of Versailles could be cast off and forgotten. The *ferme ornée*

with rustic charm was the fashion of the day and the queen recreated the atmosphere of village life. The blossoms that embellished the idyllic hamlet were far more important as an aesthetic statement than any fruit harvested, considering the nearby extensive potager (kitchen garden), which actually provided for their elaborate meals at Versailles.[50]

In the town of Cereseto in Monferrato, Italy, a traditional cherry-growing region of Italy where little interest in the crop is presently evident, a Buddhist monk named Shoryo Tarabini has begun a campaign to plant eight hundred ornamental and fruit-bearing cherry trees. Tarabini founded the Renkoji Temple in Cereseto, combining the aesthetics of East and West in a stunning and welcoming temple garden. He has recently designed a new logo for his temple and the planting project, depicting a stylized cherry blossom, a motif that is found in many Japanese family crests and popular in Japanese textiles.

Marie Antoinette-inspired portrait of Ruby Moon by photographer Beth Seliga, 2015.

Mughal Imperial poet seated in a cherry blossom garden, 1628–58.

Cherry blossoms delight all our senses. Sight, certainly, but also hearing, scent, touch and even taste. Songs about cherry blossom season, known as *sakura* songs, comprise an entire genre in Japanese music. For the Japanese, the cherry blossom season coincides with many of life's milestones. Blossoming cherries evoke a sense of new meetings, and the petals of falling cherry blossoms evoke sad goodbyes, but also bring about many memories.

Cherry blossoms are salted and pickled then steeped in boiled water to brew *sakura* blossom tea.

A traditional Japanese folk song about spring, the immediately recognizable 'Sakura, Sakura' (Cherry Blossoms, Cherry Blossoms), is the song often chosen in international settings to represent Japan. A popular melody of the Edo period (1603–1868), it was adapted as a piece for students of the koto (a traditional Japanese stringed instrument) and published in the Tokyo Academy of Music's *Collection of Japanese Koto Music*. Popular entertainers like Cat Stevens, Bon Jovi and Led Zeppelin have performed versions of 'Sakura, Sakura'. Many electronic pedestrian crossings in Japan play the melody as 'guidance music'. In 2007 *Nihon no Uta Hyakusen*, a collection of much-loved Japanese songs and nursery rhymes, included the song.[51]

The song 'Cherry Blossoms' was written in 2012 to commemorate the centennial anniversary of Japan's cherry blossom gift to Washington, DC. With a distinct Japanese feel to it, the song is both sweet and haunting, depicting the beautiful but short time that the trees are in bloom. Its melody is original, though some of the lyrics come from 'Sakura, Sakura'.

Hundreds of folk songs mention the cherry tree and cherry blossoms, including the Ukrainian song 'Oh, in the Cherry Orchard', which celebrates young love in the springtime. There was also a popular foxtrot, 'It Looks Like Rain in Cherry Blossom Lane', recorded by Canadian American bandleader Guy Lombardo in 1937.[52]

The hauntingly beautiful French political song 'Le Temps des cerises' (Cherry Time) was written in 1867, with lyrics by Jean-Baptiste Clément and music by Antoine Renard. Still popular in France, the song was originally associated with the Paris Commune, a radical socialist government that briefly ruled France in 1871. 'Cherry time' is a metaphor suggesting what life will be like after a revolution brings in social and economic changes. Adding to the romance of the song, some believed it may have been 'dedicated by the writer to a nurse who fought in the *Semaine sanglante* (Bloody Week), when French government troops overthrew the commune'.[53]

There is no doubt that cherries appeal to our sense of sight, but only a few varieties of cherry blossoms actually exude a scent. Their petals cannot be made into an essential oil, but some perfumers use aroma chemicals to recreate a cherry blossom accord, a composite scent made up of several component aroma chemicals. Cherry blossoms that do have a scent have been described as having faint lilac and rose qualities, accented with vanilla almond aromas.[54] In Leo Tolstoy's 1859 short novel *Family Happiness*, the character Masha recalls a romantic day of cherry-picking long ago:

> The scent of lilac and cherry-blossom filled the garden and the terrace, as if all the air was in bloom; it came in waves, now stronger, now weaker, so that one wanted to close one's eyes and see nothing, hear nothing, hear nothing apart from the sweet scent.[55]

As to the fruit's taste, there seems to be a universal liking for cherry flavour, but how common is it to eat cherry blossoms? Cherry blossom tea, *sakurayu*, is a Japanese herbal infusion created by steeping pickled cherry blossoms in boiled water. It is offered at weddings and other celebrations, in place of green tea. The petals are collected when the cherry trees bloom, and after the calyxes are removed the

Japanese temple sweets, *sakura wagashi,* in Kyoto, only available during cherry blossom season.

Cherry blossom motifs appear on all sorts of products during the *hanami* season throughout Japan.

petals are pickled in plum vinegar and salt, then dried and sealed in tea packets. One of the most popular sweets made and served during the cherry blossom season, *sakuramochi*, is a delicate pink-coloured rice cake carefully wrapped in a green pickled cherry tree leaf and filled with red bean paste. Widely available in lovely packaging for gifts, the treat is traditionally served on Girls' Day, *Hinamatsuri*, as well as for *hanami*.

73

During the cherry blossom season throughout Japan, virtually every product is repackaged in special wrap with lovely cherry blossom designs. There is even a *sakura*-flavoured McDonald's sandwich, served in a pale pink bun along with a Sakura McFizz.

Oddly enough, one cherry product that is difficult to obtain is cherry blossom honey. The reason for this is that when cherry blossoms bloom in early spring, bees use the nectar not so much to make honey as to expand the hive. Therefore there is only a limited supply of cherry blossom honey available on the market.

Cherry blossoms have universal appeal to all the senses and are cultivated and loved the world over. Cherry blossom festivals celebrate all that is memorable about them.

three
Fruit: From Tree to Table

You cannot buy that pleasure which it yields to him
who truly plucks it.

HENRY DAVID THOREAU, *Wild Fruits*

What is it about cherries that makes them so addictive? The size of a cherry is perfect for one bite (despite competition in the industry to create an ever larger 'super' cherry). The English claim that the small dark, almost black, cherries rescued from near extinction in the Tamar Valley in Devon are among the best tasting. Meanwhile, stunningly beautiful hybrids, designed specifically to look perfect and travel well to markets, are disappointing in taste. Officials at Britain's annual National Cherry and Soft Fruit Show use a hundred-point scale to judge the entries, with taste being just as important as appearance. A special mix of prize-winning cherries is chosen by the judge, and a container-full, called a chip basket, is immediately driven to Buckingham Palace to be presented to the queen.

Everybody seems to love cherries, from the child who 'scrumps' a ripe cherry from a neighbour's tree to the queen of England. Because of their short growing season and brief shelf life, cherries are expensive compared to other fruits. One cannot eat a cherry delicately and politely. As Edward Bunyard states in his 1934 edition of *The Anatomy of Dessert*, 'The black, finger-staining, napkin-ruining juice makes it perhaps a fruit for garden strolls rather than for the decorous dessert.'[1]

While early paintings often show aristocrats harvesting cherries in their best clothes, the harvesting depicted was more for entertainment than true agricultural practice. A well-known and popular porcelain pattern from the eighteenth century known as 'The Cherry Pickers' illustrates a Rococo romantic scene of lovers enjoying a particularly delightful picnic experience, rather than a day's hard work. Timing is critical when harvesting cherries. Bunyard suggests, 'one must walk through the orchard a fortnight after the crop has been gathered, and here and there a fruit which has been missed will reveal to the gleaner what a cherry really may be.'[2]

Heritage cherries, Tamar Valley, Devon, UK.

Queen Elizabeth II reviewing the prize-winning entries at the National Fruit
Collection Cherry Fair, Kent, UK, 1989.

Cherries are a non-climacteric fruit, that is, they do not continue
to ripen once they have been picked. A fully ripe cherry cannot withstand long shipping and storage times. On the last days of ripening,
cherries can increase their sugar content up to 25 per cent, so they
should not be harvested too soon. However, waiting too long poses
the risk of losing the crop to birds. Farmers closely observe ripening
clues such as taste, colour, firmness, size and the ease with which the
cherries come off the tree (pedicel-fruit retention force) to determine
the optimal time to harvest their cherries. Today, orchard managers
are aided by scientific instruments to help determine when the cherries are ripe and ready to harvest. For example, refractometers can
be used to measure Brix levels (an indicator of sugar levels) and other
specialized instruments can be used to measure size, firmness, colour
and the pedicel-fruit retention force.

Harvesting technique is critical. Pickers must be careful not to
tear off the woody fruit spur, which continues to produce fruit each
year. However, harvesting must be done as quickly as possible if it is
going to rain, as rain causes cherries, especially sweet cherries, to split.

Throughout history cherries have been harvested by hand, a task traditionally requiring ladders since the trees can grow up to 18 metres (60 ft) tall. Harvesters often used special baskets that were either worn or tied on ropes to facilitate handling the harvested cherries. The current trend is to plant dwarf trees, which permit safer and quicker harvesting. Chemicals such as ethephon (Ethrel) can be applied to the trees to loosen cherries for harvesting.

Harvesting cherries is a labour-intensive business. Faced with increasing competition and shortages of harvesters, the cherry industry is continually seeking to improve harvest efficiency without

'Cherry Pickers' pattern adapted from a porcelain tea service made in China for the Western market between 1750 and 1775.

Dorothea Lange, *Cherry Pickers near Millville, New Jersey*, June 1936.

compromising the quality of the fruit. Current research focuses on better integration of the entire value chain, from genetics and breeding to processing and marketing, keeping in mind the needs and preferences of consumers.

Mechanized harvest systems, including 'shake and catch', have been developed and are used extensively with sour cherries as these are mostly processed rather than sold fresh. The tree is mechanically shaken and the ripe cherries fall into a cushioned catcher pan. The tree must be shaken in such a way as not to damage it while all the ripe cherries are harvested.

After the cherries are picked and gathered they are sorted and sized, either by hand or electronically with computer scanning and sorting technology. They are packed for either fresh market sales or commercial processing. Since cherries do not ripen further after picking, and sour cherries spoil quickly, it is critical that they are sold or processed (juiced, frozen, canned or dried) within a day or two of their picking. In the U.S. 99 per cent of sour cherries are processed rather than sold fresh. For sweet cherries the figure is 24 per cent, with 76 per cent sold fresh.[3]

Fresh, sweet cherries have a shorter storage and shelf life than most other commercial fruits such as apples or pears. Keeping the cherries cold from harvest to sale, referred to as the 'cold chain', is the best way to ensure delivery of a quality product to the end-user. Being susceptible to bruising, cherries require extra care on the packing line to minimize damage.

Packing options include wooden boxes, cartons, plastic clamshells, punnets (small boxes) and bags. Current research is being conducted into novel compostable packaging and bio-based containers with micro-perforated lids. The goal of the research is to develop packaging that will help cherries withstand extended shipping times of up to 25 days from harvest to retail sale, for example when selling Chilean cherries to China.

In the past, because of the difficulty in growing and marketing cherries, farmers typically sold their produce to local consumers. Family members would bring the cherries to town to sell in either local markets or directly on the streets. Even today, roadside stands typically appear in areas where cherries are grown.

Cherries are now being marketed as a 'superfood', with health benefits such as helping to improve sleep, prevent cancer and soothe sore muscles. Marketers always attempt to make their cherries look as attractive as possible, sometimes even waxing them. Research has focused on how to make cherry stems keep their green colour, an indicator the consumer may look for to judge freshness. Cherries are often chosen based on their colour or size, though these qualities might not necessarily translate into a better taste.

Modern marketing practice has changed the way cherries are sold. In Portugal detailed market research has found that consumers in some parts of the country prefer certain shades of red in the cherries they purchase. Marketing techniques that specify the cherry

Machinery for washing and sorting cherries. Fundaō, Portugal.

variety, or the country Designation of Origin, are often used to project exclusivity and attain a higher selling price. The first trademark in France for cherries, 'Les Montes de Venasque', was designated in 1978.[4]

Globally, cherry growers are continually trying to develop new export markets. The reverse season in the Southern Hemisphere brings cherries from Australia, New Zealand and South America to European and North American markets in December and January. The Chilean Fruit Exporters Association notes that in 2017–18

Cherry liqueurs, wines and beverages.

over 90 per cent of Chile's exported cherries supplied the Chinese market.[5] Chilean cherries ripen just in time for the Chinese New Year. To the Chinese, the auspicious red colour of cherries symbolizes prosperity and fortune, and the cherries' roundness symbolizes perfection and eternity.

An example of a marketing campaign is Fresh Cherry, an informational and promotional programme partially financed by the Republic of Bulgaria and the European Union (EU), and targeting the markets of the Middle East (Saudi Arabia and the United Arab Emirates) and Belarus. Its goal is to inform professionals and consumers about the attractive characteristics of cherries, particularly their health benefits, and increase interest in their consumption.

In 2008 the British government established 16 July as National Cherry Day, in conjunction with its Cherry Aid campaign to promote the growing and consumption of the British cherry. Two goals of this campaign are to save local varieties of cherries from extinction and to increase the number of cherry orchards after years of decline.

All of the packing, shipping and marketing can be bypassed if one grows cherries for personal use or goes to a 'pick your own' orchard, or a farm stand. In Kent, England, one can even rent a cherry tree, giving urbanites the opportunity for an agricultural experience.

It is generally agreed that cherries are best eaten fresh, but numerous ways of preserving cherries have been developed so they may also be enjoyed outside of their short growing season. A time-honoured method of preserving fruit is to make wine. In most countries (outside the EU) wine is legally defined as any beverage made from fermented fruit, including cherries, with an alcohol content of at least 8 per cent but no more than 14 per cent. If fresh fruit is not available, cherry juice, syrup or concentrate can be used for cherry wine-making.

Cherry wine is usually made with tart cherries, as that variety provides a higher level of acids, although sometimes a blend of sweet and sour cherries is used. The indigenous people of North America made chokecherry wine. Cherry wines can also be used to make fortified wines and liqueurs, which are sweetened alcoholic drinks with various flavours, oils and extracts added. Historically, liqueurs were referred to as cordials and were often used medicinally. Brandy is an alcoholic drink produced by distilling wine (35–60 per cent alcohol by volume). *The Cook's Oracle*, first published in 1817 by William Kitchiner, mentions the use of cherry brandy in making calves' feet jelly.

Ginjinha, or simply *ginja*, is a Portuguese liqueur made by infusing sour cherries into brandy, then adding sugar and cinnamon. In the Portuguese town of Óbidos, *ginja* is commonly served in a small edible chocolate cup. The sour cherry brandy that Romanians make, often in their own homes, is called *visinata*. Two versions of a cherry alcoholic drink are enjoyed in both Portugal and Romania: a clear, stronger drink for the men, and a red-coloured, sweeter, fruitier option preferred by women.

Similar to *visinata*, *ratafia* is a cherry liqueur of French Creole origin. It is made by soaking ripe cherries in alcohol for several days, then adding a sugar syrup to encourage fermentation. Cherry bounce is an American version popularized by Martha Washington in the eighteenth century.

Heering Cherry is a Danish liqueur created by Peter Frederik Heering and first sold in 1818. It is typically made from unpitted dark-red, sour cherries called 'stevns'; the inclusion of cherry pits gives it an almond flavour. Heering Cherry Liqueur was popularized in 1915 as an ingredient in the Singapore Sling cocktail.[6]

Kirschwasser, or simply *kirsch*, is an unsweetened cherry brandy that originated in Germany. It is made from the distilled juice of black cherries with the addition of crushed cherry stones, giving it a slight 'almond' flavour. This colourless liqueur is an important ingredient in Black Forest cake.

There are also popular cherry beers and ales, such as *kriek*, made in Belgium. Microbreweries in the U.S. are experimenting with cherry beers and ales as speciality or seasonal offerings.

Artisanal cherry liqueurs and sweets at Pyana Vyshnya, Drunk Cherry bar, Lviv, Ukraine.

Jams and preserves made from historical recipes using cherries from the gardens of Thomas Jefferson and George Washington.

Maraschino cherries date back several centuries to the coastal regions of Slovenia, Croatia, Bosnia, Herzegovina, Serbia, and northern Italy, where a liqueur was manufactured from a local cherry called the 'Marasca'. In 1896 U.S. manufacturers began experimenting with a domestic light-skinned sweet cherry called the 'Royal Ann'. During Prohibition in the U.S., alcohol was banned and therefore unavailable to be used to make traditional maraschino cherries. A process to make a non-alcoholic American version was developed in which the cherries are brined in a solution of calcium salts, and artificial flavourings and colouring agents then added.[7]

Another method of preserving cherries is to dry them. This process is particularly important when working with chokecherries as they become sweeter and their astringency vanishes when dried. Native Americans frequently added dried, powdered chokecherries to meat when making pemmican, a concentrated mix of fat and

American and Italian versions of maraschino cherries.

protein. Chokecherries have acids that helped to naturally preserve the buffalo meat. Pemmican was a 'travel food' for them, as it would remain edible for a long time. The Ojibwa sometimes ground dried wild cherries into a flour and used it for soup. The journals of U.S. explorers Lewis and Clark's expedition from 1804 to 1806 mention eating 'a Kettle of boild Simnins, beans, Corn & Choke Cherries'.[8]

When dried, sour cherries tend to hold their colour and texture better than sweet cherries, so they are used commercially in cooking and preservative processes such as freezing and canning. Dried cherries can be plain or have salt, sugar or preservatives added and are used in both sweet and savoury dishes. They are often added into trail mix for health benefits and natural sweetness.

Sugar has long been used in food preservation. When added to foods, it binds to the water content, reducing the amount of water available for the growth of microorganisms. Ancient Greeks often preserved fruits in honey. Apicius advises, 'select them [cherries] all very carefully with the stems on and place them in honey so they do not touch each other.'[9] Specialist in sustainable agriculture Mark Shepard describes the process of continuing the tradition of preserving cherries in honey in his 2013 book *Restoration Agriculture*.[10]

The fourteenth-century Catalonian book *Líbre de totes maneres de confits* contains recipes for cherry candied fruits and jams. As early as 1365, the trade unions (syndicates) of Apt in Provence, France, offered candied fruit to Pope Urban V. Thus the city of Apt became known as the world capital of candied fruit. Its manufacture is a long and expensive process, so the most beautiful fruits are chosen, particularly the 'Bigarreaux' variety grown in Provence. In 1868 Mathieu Wood, an English businessman then travelling in Provence, discovered the candied fruit from the Apt region and helped introduce it to the English market, where it remains a popular confectionery.

In the nineteenth century the British love of the outdoors and the vogue for picnicking and camping created a preference for food that was easier to carry than the traditional pudding. The fruitcake, to which candied fruits and French glacé cherries were added, became popular and an important part of British baking culture.

In 1555 the physician and reputed seer Michel de Notredame, or Nostradamus as he is better known, published instructions detailing how to preserve cherries. The method is still successful today, but note that nearly 1 kilogram (2 lb) of the finest cherries will produce barely a half-cup of jelly, though if done correctly it will be as 'beautiful as a ruby', as Nostradamus promises.[11]

First Lady Martha Washington's eighteenth-century *Booke of Cookery* and *Booke of Sweetmeats* has a preserved cherry recipe. Hannah Glasse's *Art of Cookery*, first published in Dublin in 1748 and in America in 1805, and the 1851 edition of Eliza Leslie's *Directions for Cookery*, published in Philadelphia, contain similar recipes for preserving cherries.

In the gourmet food world, artisanal foods are gaining popularity. Small-batch producers use traditional recipes that help preserve the heritage of local fruit varieties that cannot be grown in the quantities

Glazed candied cherries produced in Provence are designated in the National Inventory of Intangible Cultural Heritage in France.

necessary for commercial jam production. Some larger producers like Borde, in Saugues in France's Loire Valley, have adopted artisanal cherry jam recipes for the larger markets. Wilkin & Sons, established in 1885 in Tiptree, Essex, is the holder of the Royal Warrant to provide jams for the British royal household, including cherry jam.

In Bologna, Italy, in 1905 Gennaro Fabbri developed what came to be known as the Fabbri Amarena cherry. He and his wife, Rachele, ran a general store in Portomaggiore near an Amarena cherry orchard. Rachele picked the cherries and slow-cooked and semi-candied them. So pleased was Gennaro with this sweet treat that he bought a beautiful blue-and-white ceramic jar from a local artist to hold the cherries.[12] Fabbri Company, which today is the world's largest producer of preserved Amarena cherries, continues to market them in its unmistakable trademark blue-and-white jar. They are enjoyed as a topping for gelato, or ice cream, cakes and other desserts, and also in a variety of savoury dishes.

Amarena cherries in the iconic blue-and-white jar of Fabbri, the world's largest producer.

Salt, like sugar, draws moisture out of foods and prevents micro-organisms from growing. In Giresun, Turkey, considered by some to be the place where cherries originated, salted cherries of the local sour cherry variety are used in a popular savoury dish called *tuzlusu kavurmesi*. An Iranian snackfood is *albaloo hoshk*, salted dried sour cherries. The *American Food Journal* in 1913 included a recipe for salting unripe cherries.

Salt and vinegar are the two necessary ingredients to pickle a fruit or vegetable. The practice of pickling dates to about 2030 BCE, when cucumbers were first pickled in India. Pickling spread around the world, particularly in eastern Europe, where Jews created kosher dill pickles.[13] In Poland, Russia and Ukraine, it was common to pickle beetroot, shredded cabbage and cherries. Ukrainian pickled cherries are available at speciality food stores and make a unique addition to charcuterie plates.

Homemade pickled cherries from traditional family recipes, Szentalszlo, Romania.

Another way to preserve cherries is to can them. About 22 per cent of sour cherries are canned, with the rest being frozen, juiced or processed for industrial cherry products. A popular sour-cherry canned product is cherry pie filling, of which Comstock is the world's largest commercial producer. Sweet cherries do not lend themselves well to canning, as they do not retain their shape and flavour through the process. The sweet cherry variety 'Royal Ann' cans the most successfully.

Cherries can also be preserved through a process known as lacto-fermentation, during which desirable microorganisms are deliberately introduced. In *Nourishing Traditions*, cookbook author Sally Fallon offers a cherry chutney recipe that uses fresh, uncooked cherries and whey.

Producers are experimenting with cherries or cherry flavourings added to a variety of new products, such as salsa, chutney, barbecue sauce and balsamic vinegars. Cherries have been added to sausage products and ground beef to increase their nutritional value. Cherries can be substituted in some products for tomatoes, such as in cherry ketchup. The u.s. National Aeronautics and Space Administration (NASA) developed a semi-dehydrated cherry bar for the 1972 *Apollo 16* mission, to be eaten directly from the package with no reconstitution required.

Many of these products may not contain actual cherries. Sometimes cherry flavouring is added to simulate the taste of the real fruit. Billionaire businessman and spokesman for Cherry Coke Warren Buffett drinks the beverage every day. The soft drink, which contains no real cherries, is popular worldwide; beverage cans in China have Buffett's picture on them.[14] One of the most popular flavours of Lifesaver sweets is cherry, although here too there are no real cherries in them.

Actually, artificial cherry flavouring doesn't taste all that much like real cherries. Accurate imitations of cherry reportedly taste uninteresting and weak. Artificial cherry flavouring tastes more like an imitation of maraschino cherries, which themselves are made from artificial flavourings. There are many formulations of artificial cherry

Cherry-flavoured condensed milk, a popular sweetener for coffee in Belarus.

flavour depending on who the buyers are, such as candy manufacturers or pharmaceutical companies. They are used in liquid medicines to mask the unpleasant bitter taste of the drugs they contain. One benefit for companies that use them is that artificial cherry flavourings are cheap, easy to make and have a familiar taste.

According to food specialists, many fruits have natural flavour companions. Cherries pair well with other fruits, wines and a variety of nuts. They also pair well with cheeses such as Camembert; meats such as duck, pork and foie gras; and herbs and spices such as coriander (cilantro), basil, mint, thyme, vanilla, black peppercorn, chilli and cinnamon. Cherries and chocolate is one of the most famous combinations, especially as chocolate-covered cherries, which not only combine two delicious flavours but have cultural associations with love, romance and sex.

One great way to experience the extensive variety of flavourful cherry products is to visit any one of the numerous cherry blossom and fruit festivals held all around the world.

Who wouldn't want two birthday parties every year? Both the blossoming and harvesting of cherries have been, and continue to be, cause for exuberant celebrations every year, virtually everywhere they are grown. From events that go back hundreds of years, such as traditional Japanese *hanami*, to brand-new events designed by hard-working tourist offices to highlight new initiatives or revive old ones, there are a host of stakeholders hoping to create economic and entertainment opportunities for their communities. Festivals, carnivals and fairs are important forms of social and cultural participation and are ways of articulating shared values.

Harvest festivals celebrate foods from the crops that come to maturity at the time of the festival. In the U.S. pies made from fresh cherries traditionally appear at cherry festivals; there are even

Chocolate-covered cherry cordials, Shanes Confectionary, Philadelphia.

cherry-pie baking and pie-eating contests. At cherry festivals in Portugal cherries are added to the national pastry, *pastel de nata*.

Abundant food from the harvest and the high spirits of free time after successfully completing it are two central features of these festivals. Eating, contests, music and romance are common at harvest festivals around the world. The July cherry harvest coincides with other national celebrations like Canada Day (1 July), U.S.

Cherry tarts, *pastel cereja*, Paris Pastelaria, Fundão, Portugal.

Traditional Romanian cherry soup, which includes a cloud of meringue and cinnamon, prepared by Vera Keleman.

Independence Day (4 July) and Bastille Day (14 July), and the red fruits often play a part in the feasting.

Adam Gollner in *Fruit Hunters* (2008), writes that anthropologists have documented fruit-fuelled group sex among tribes all over the world as part of religious festivals and holidays. Religion historian Mircea Eliade suggests that 'Communal fruit sex was a fact of life in early agrarian societies . . . a prime opportunity to unleash an orgy.'[15]

Cherry festival procession with members of the Brotherhood of the Cherries in traditional costume, Venasque, France.

In Jane Grigson's *Fruit Book*, the English writer describes festival traditions that began in the Middle Ages and continue to this day:

> People wandered about the orchards; the fruit was picked and sold; there was dancing, drinking, and making love (a few years ago – this was written in 1982 – there were still some old people in our Wiltshire village with birthdays nine months after the Clyffe feast, which took place every year at cherry time).[16]

In July each year a cherry festival is held at Brogdale Collections in Faversham, Kent, home to the UK's National Fruit Collection. This location includes over 60 hectares (150 ac) of farmland. Brogdale is a living-history museum of more than 4,000 varieties of fruit trees. Brogdale Collections, owned by the UK Department for Environment, Food and Rural Affairs (Defra), offers public access to an affordable fruit identification service with professional fruit experts and is part of an international programme to protect plant genetic resources for the future. In a nod to the historical agrarian roots of Britain, the Worshipful Company of Fruiterers has been actively supporting the fruit industry since the thirteenth century. Their mission is to promote excellence and support education and research within the fruit industry. They choose the prize-winning entries at the festival and make the awards.

The earliest cherries harvested in France are celebrated at the cherry festival in the historic town of Céret, in the department of Pyrénées-Orientales in southwest France, near the Franco-Spanish border. A tradition was established in 1932 that the first cherries picked at Céret are sent to the president of France. Currently, the Céret Cherry Festival takes place in late May.[17] There is an entire local gastronomic heritage based on the fruit, which is used in pies, jams, jellies, a delicious brandy and even beers and liqueurs. Celebrations include cherry tastings and special cherry menus in local restaurants, stoning, and stone-spitting competitions, and traditional Catalan *bandas* and *Sardana* dancing.

Another colourful cherry festival is held annually in the French Provençal town of Venasque. It includes a parade of local growers dressed in historical costume, members of the Brotherhood of the Cherries, proudly displaying the first fruits of their harvest. A highlight is the *clafoutis* competition, featuring varieties of this French quiche-like version of the cherry pie. The exceptionally sweet flavour and large size of 'Les Monts de Venasque' (also nicknamed 'Red Diamond') cherries are due to the unique climate and soil of the local orchards. According to the Venasque tourism website, 'They [the cherries] are carefully picked by hand in our area. They bask in the sun 4,800 hours per year, and are screened by hand for size (minimum 26 millimetres) and quality.'[18] There are 21 towns on the Cherry

Route of the Monts de Venasque, a route that visits cherry orchards and producers stretching from Ventoux to Luberon.

In Bisceglie and Turi, cities of the Puglia region, Italy, Sagra della Ciliegia Ferrovia festival is held each June in honour of the 'Railway Cherry', a strain developed from the seeds of a tree growing near the railway lines from Sammichele di Bari in around 1935. In Pecetto Torinese, near the northern Italian city of Turin, the cherry festival features cherries that have been recognized for their fine quality ever since they were first offered at the 1911 International Exhibition. They are also included as 'Typical Products of the Province of Turin'.

Cherry growing is an important agricultural activity in Chile and Argentina, where the growing season is from November through January. A festival has been held annually since 1991 in the town of Los Antiguos in Patagonia, Chile. As well as providing entertainment for the local cherry growers, it aims at attracting tourists and includes tours of the farms, dancing and feasting on homemade cherry pastries and cakes.

Two of the world's most significant current producers of cherries are Turkey and Iran, and festivals in each of these countries attract local attention. The village of Kirazli, Turkey, was founded in 1427 when three families of travelling shepherds discovered that the lush, green area provided ideal pastureland for their sheep. The incredibly fertile soil and perfect growing climate were ideal for cultivating fruit trees. Because of the importance to the area of the local cherry crop, the village is named Kirazli, meaning 'cherry land' in Turkish. Kirazli has held a cherry festival in June of every year since 1975.[19] The village, and the Kirazli Village Ecological Life Association, has also been developing and running ecological agriculture projects since 2004, focusing mainly on sustainability.

While orchards in Iran have been producing cherries for centuries, the country's First National Festival of Cherry was held in 2016 to encourage worldwide interest and production. Iranians are avid connoisseurs of cherries; their annual per capita consumption of 3 kilograms (6½ lb) is double that of the U.S. Khorasan Razavi, west Azerbaijan, east Azerbaijan, Isfahan and Semnan are the main producing areas and exporters of Iranian cherries. The principal export destinations are Iraq, Azerbaijan, Russia and Arab countries.

An unexpected place to find a cherry festival is in the Atlas Mountains town of Sefrou in Morocco. Included in the United Nations list of Intangible Cultural Heritage of Humanity in 2012, the cherry festival here involves the celebration of the fruit harvest highlighted by the pageantry, entertainment and local craftsmanship around the choosing and presentation of the Cherry Queen. This competition draws both local and national competitors. Local craftswomen make elaborate silk buttons for the traditional dress for the Cherry Queen, and sports clubs participate, along with music and dance troupes, in a celebration that is a source of much local pride.

In the U.S. many would rank the National Cherry Festival as the ultimate celebration of cherries. The event is held every year in July in what is locally known as the 'Cherry Capital of the World', Traverse City, Michigan. It began in 1910 as a celebration of cherry blossoms but gradually morphed into a showcase for the fruit.

Another U.S. event takes place in Salem, Oregon, which held an annual cherry blossom festival from 1903 through 1968, with a king 'Bing', a queen and a royal court. A group called the 'Cherrians', organized in 1913, was designated to watch the cherry trees every year and, a couple of weeks before the peak of cherry blossoms, would set the Sunday for the annual Cherry Blossom Day. More recently, the festival has been revived, revised, and sponsored by the Japan–American Society of Oregon. It includes a 5-kilometre (8 mi.) Cherry Blossom Run, with performances, workshops and demonstrations that share and celebrate Japanese culture. It also features cherry food product samples created in this traditional cherry-growing region of the U.S.

While the beauty of the blossoms and the desire for the delicious fruit never change, festivals are by no means static events, and the activities offered to the communities evolve over time. One perhaps peculiar, though fun, activity at cherry festivals is a cherry-stone-spitting contest. Participants compete to see who can spit a cherry stone (or pit) the furthest. In 2003 American 'Young Gun' Krause set the current all-time record for the longest distance in the International Cherry Pit Spitting Championship with a distance of 28.51 metres (93 ft 6½ in.).[20] 'Young Gun' took the championship from his father, 'Pellet Gun' Krause, a ten-time champion. While it may be thought that cherry-stone-spitting contests are an American invention, there are records showing that a game called cherry-pit, in which contestants spat the stone into a hole, was known in Elizabethan England. In Shakespeare's *Twelfth Night*, Sir Toby Belch says, "Tis not for gravity to play at cherry-pit with Satan.' Stone-spitting contests are also held at cherry festivals in Switzerland and New Zealand.

Native Americans used cherry stones as dice in games of chance, but also as a food source. Although the stones contain toxic prussic acid, they found various methods to neutralize the poison by boiling them, grinding or mashing them and creating cherry stone meal, which was then shaped into balls.

Cherry stones are sometimes called pips, pits or seeds. The kernel within the stone contains prussic acid, but this is rarely a problem if consumed since stones cannot be broken down by enzymes in the human digestive tract. Swallowing a broken stone could be more problematic, but even then it would take a large number of them to become a health hazard. More likely, someone, especially a child, could choke on a cherry stone. Unstoned cherries should not be given to children under the age of four.

In 1905 a German physician named Max Nassauer published *Der Gute Doktor: ein Nützlich Bilderbuch für Kinder und Eltern* (The Good Doctor: A Useful Picture Book for Children and Parents), which contained fourteen cautionary medical tales for children. In one of them, 'Franz the Pip Swallower', a young boy eats unwashed, unripe fruits, including cherries, experiences terrible cramps and falls to the ground 'and was like dead'. Luckily for little Franz:

The 2018 cherry-stone-spitting champion T. J. Mason, Cherry Festival, Traverse City, Michigan.

The doctor came, took a tube,
Sticks it into Franz's tummy
And takes this, horror of horrors,
Twelve cherry pips out.
If the doctor was not there,
Franz would be living nevermore.

The late American humorist Erma Bombeck was not talking about swallowing cherry stones when she wrote *If Life Is a Bowl of Cherries, What Am I Doing in the Pits?* She was equating them with the darker side of life. American slang says, 'It's the pits,' when referring to something negative.

Unstoned cherries continue to be used in *clafoutis*. Traditional recipes for homemade cherry jam suggested simmering a muslin bag of cherry stones in a pot of cherries and sugar. *Mahlab* is a spice made

French cherry pie, *clafouti*, Venasque, France.

from the kernels within the cherry stones from the *Prunus mahaleb* tree. This spice is a staple in Middle Eastern cuisine. The flavouring is frequently used in sweetbreads such as Turkish *çörek*, Greek *tsoureki* and Armenian *chorak*.

Most dishes utilizing cherries are served with the stones removed. Unless one has a cherry stoner, getting this done is a tedious and messy process. Cherry producers have developed elaborate machinery that automatically removes the stones quickly and efficiently. Chefs in restaurants and home makers do not have access to such machinery, and so sometimes come up with inventive ways to remove stones. Poking the stone through with chopsticks, pastry tips or straws is one method. An unbent paper clip, toothpick or lobster- or crab-picking tool may be inserted into the stem end of the cherry, then twisted around the stone, pushing it out. A simple cherry stoner can also be constructed from an old fork (see the YouTube video cited at the end of this book).

Cherry stones have been used in various cultures as magical or divination tools. In a scene from the popular movie *The Witches of Eastwick* (1987), the witches spat cherry stones into a bowl, enacting a curse. In folk medicine, cloth bags stuffed with cherry stones can

Vintage cherry stoner, early 1900s.

be heated and applied to the body like a heating pad. The bags are also helpful in aromatherapy, as they give off a light cherry fragrance.

Cherry stones have even been turned into artworks. Indigenous peoples strung them as necklaces and, in modern times, some sculptors have created amazing miniature carvings from them. Bob Shamey, of Ligonier, Pennsylvania, is one such carver who sculpts stones from a variety of fruits, especially cherry; his work has twice been cited in *Ripley's Believe It or Not.*

The centre of the stone, the kernel, also has some useful applications. Because it is high in antioxidants, oleic acid and natural emollients, kernel oil helps moisturize dry skin and is used in massages.

Archaeologists and ethnobotanists have used cherry stones to determine what food people ate in ancient times, as well as to trace the origin and distribution of cherries. Archaeological evidence suggests that Roman soldiers garrisoned at a fort in Wales ate cherries and blackberries. Cherry stones resembling those of modern sour cherries have been excavated at several sites in England, including Silchester, Selsey, West Wittering and also near the Thames in London.[21]

Even cherry stems have some value other than merely holding the cherry to the tree. Stems brewed into tea are said to offer various medicinal properties, including relieving menstrual cramps, but the brew can simply be enjoyed as a soothing beverage.

An infamous bar trick is to ask someone to tie a cherry stem into a knot using their tongue. This is not easy to do, and it takes quite a bit of lingual dexterity to be successful. But, in keeping with the romantic persona of the cherry, the person who can successfully tie a knot with his or her tongue is perceived as being an accomplished lover.

The Guinness World Record for the most cherry stems knotted with the tongue is held by Al Gliniecki. He can tie fourteen stems in one minute, 39 in three minutes, and 911 in one hour. As reported in the *New York Times*, Gliniecki gives this advice:

Take the stem and lay it lengthwise down the center of your tongue. Close your lips. Bend your tongue upward, pinning it against the roof of your mouth. This movement will fold the stem in half and leave the two ends crossed and facing forward. Choose stalks with bulbous tips, so your tongue can more easily locate an end and push it through the loop.[22]

As entertaining as tying knots with the tongue may be, most people are quite happy simply to be able to enjoy cherries, with or without stems.

four

Wood: Everlasting Beauty

It was the best disaster ever to happen to Pennsylvania.

In the 1700s, when settlers first ventured into Penn's Woods, now known as Pennsylvania, they found the mountain-top forests thick with towering white pine trees. A straight-grained knotless tree, the pine was perfect for masts and spars used to build Yankee clipper ships. By the nineteenth century the lumber industry in Pennsylvania was in full swing, but it all came crashing down in the early 1900s as excessive logging stripped Pennsylvania of almost all its forests of pine, leaving millions of hectares of bare hillsides.

The destructive harvesting of the pine trees turned out to be a stroke of good luck for other trees. Hardwood trees, including cherry, grow best in sunlight and, with the taller pine trees eliminated, the hardwoods flourished. 'What we really have is a freak accident,' said James R. Grace, assistant professor of forestry at Pennsylvania State University. 'The fact that we got a valuable hardwood forest back is pure luck.'[2]

The clear-cutting of the pine forest that subsequently enabled cherry trees to flourish was indeed a stroke of luck, but that was an unusual circumstance. Today, good forestry practice prohibits clear-cutting in favour of selective logging. Because cherry trees have little tolerance for shade, cherry saplings do not do well under the relatively undisturbed canopy of a forest being managed through

Forest of black cherry trees (*Prunus serotina*), McConnellsville, New York.

selective cutting. As a result, there is an ever-diminishing supply of cherry wood in the wild.

One of the most valuable hardwoods to take advantage of this new environmental opportunity was black cherry, *Prunus serotina*, earning Pennsylvania the title 'black cherry capital of the world'.[3] The top-grade black cherry found in the state is highly prized in the manufacture of elegant furniture because of its rich colour, distinct

German mechanical architect's desk designed by Abraham Roentgen featuring cherry-wood veneer, c. 1780–95.

grain and malleable texture. Lumber buyers from all over the world, especially Belgium, Canada, France, Germany, Italy, Japan and Taiwan, are big buyers of Pennsylvania cherry wood. Some cherry-wood logs can cost as much as $800–$900 each.

Such an extravagant price for cherry wood would have surprised eighteenth-century New England furniture makers who used the wood of their fruiting cherry trees that they had brought over from England. They called this 'New England Mahogany', to imitate fashionable Honduran mahogany.[4] People of means, such as Thomas Jefferson, sometimes used cherry wood for flooring. The parquet floor of the reception room he designed in his Monticello home was modelled on a French example he had seen on his travels, and was constructed of cherry and beech, two contrasting woods.[5] Contemporary flooring companies offer a Monticello-style parquet option today that highlights the contrasting wood colours.

Cherry wood is often used in cabinetry and furniture because dramatically different grain contrasts can often be found in one solid cut. This means that finished products can range in colour from a light pinkish brown to a medium reddish brown; time and exposure to light will also darken the shade. Furniture makers and woodcarvers also appreciate the fact that cherry wood is durable, easy to work with, and takes a finish well.

Abraham Roentgen (1711–1793), a German furniture maker, crafted cherry wood furniture with clever hidden compartments and movable elements. There is a beautiful writing and card table, with mechanical action allowing it to serve multiple purposes, in the Victoria & Albert Museum in London. A desk with hidden compartments can also be found in the Metropolitan Museum of Art in New York. These pieces feature cherry wood, particularly because of its beautiful colour. British furniture makers such as Charles Barr prefer the more expensive American cherry wood over the European species because it offers wider board sizes with fewer faults and defects.

Harden Furniture, founded in 1844 in McConnellsville, New York, still uses solid hardwoods, especially cherry, in the manufacture of quality furniture. The company manages 4,000 hectares (10,000 ac), using environmentally sound principles to grow their own trees. Harden Furniture provided a new cherry conference table for the White House, and also created office furniture for the First Lady's office as well as executive desks for the Executive Office Building in Washington, DC. They also made 1,000 cherry wood chairs for both the Capitol Visitor Center and the caucus rooms in the U.S. House and Senate.[6]

President Barack Obama seated at a Harden cherry-wood table in the White House, Washington, DC, 2010.

In 1944 the Japanese American sculptor and artist Isamu Noguchi designed several classic furniture pieces which he created in cherry wood. The simple design of his Modway Triangular Coffee Table has only three elements: a glass top supported by two interlocking cherry wood base pieces. It has become an icon of extraordinary harmony between form and function and continues to be manufactured by Herman Miller, a renowned furniture maker.[7] Another famous Japanese American woodworker and architect who often created unique pieces made with cherry wood, George Katsutoshi Nakashima (1905–1990), was one of the leading innovators of twentieth-century furniture design. Nakashima was honoured by the emperor and government of Japan in 1983 when he received the Order of the Sacred Treasure.[8]

Craftsmen at the Thomas Moser Company in Auburn, Maine, use cherry wood for many of their handcrafted pieces. Moser artisans created their simple and elegant Harpswell cherry armchair for Pope Benedict's visit to the U.S. in 2008, and another for Pope Francis's visit to the U.S. in 2015. The chair designed for Pope Francis was later auctioned for charity.[9]

A community of Roman Catholic monks belonging to the Order of Cistercians of the Strict Observance, commonly known as Trappists, has found a unique use for cherry wood. At their abbey in New Melleray, Iowa, they harvest it from trees they manage on their grounds and fashion it into simple wooden caskets and burial urns of high quality. The abbey's website explains their purpose in creating the caskets:

> By providing grieving families with a simple, beautiful casket prayerfully crafted and blessed by monks, we not only console God's heartbroken children, but give delight to the Lord himself whose teaching he sees fulfilled with ardent love and care . . . we find meaning in the fact as carpenters, we are somehow in solidarity with Jesus and Joseph who earned their livelihood this way.[10]

Because cherry wood is evenly textured, straight-grained and has a beautiful colour, it has been a favourite material for woodcarvers when creating smaller pieces. Throughout the world, there are many cultures with a tradition of woodcarving, and their work is often

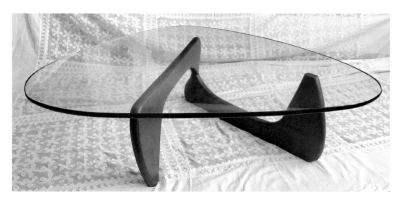

Noguchi Modway triangular table of cherry wood and glass, designed in 1944, still in production.

Cherry-wood crafts featuring attractive wood grains.

featured at festivals worldwide. For example, each June in Coruia, Romania, a festival organized by a local folk group, Cireşarii (Black Cherry), displays the traditional local artefacts, including cherry woodcarvings.

Romania is a country where woodcarving still flourishes today. Some Romanian woodworkers use cherry wood to produce household items such as wooden spoons, plates, spindles, looms and pipes. Romanian homes often feature ornate gates carved of cherry. This folk art is a cherished tradition, and children often participate in woodcarving classes.

The Romanian woodcarver Mark Tudose carves spoons that carry traditional Romanian designs. He says:

My idea is to try to make an apparently simple object valuable through its story and the symbols behind the story. In life,

Harpswell chair designed by Thomas Moser for Pope Francis's visit to the U.S. in 2015, with hand-embroidered logo of the World Meeting of Families.

people search, consciously or unconsciously, for just a couple of simple things: love, happiness, luck, wisdom . . . With my spoons, I am telling Romanian folk tales which deal with these spiritual elements.[11]

The Wooden Spoons Museum (Muzeul Lingurilor de lemn – Ion Tugui) in Câmpulung Moldovenesc, Romania, contains more than 6,000 examples of wooden spoons, many of them made from cherry wood. In addition to the usual tablespoons, it displays more unusual designs used to commemorate betrothals, marriages and deaths. There is even an 'avaricious' spoon, with the bowl so flat that only

Traditional carved cherry wood spoons, Romania.

Cherry burl bowl made by Douglas Richard, Squirrelywood, Welaka, Florida.

a little food can be placed in it, and a 'nagging woman' spoon with a wooden ring attached to it to be shaken at the offending wife.

In the United States, woodcarver Jonathan Simons of Jonathan's Wild Cherry Spoons, Kempton, Pennsylvania, has discovered the value of cherry wood in his craft. Simons originally made his spoons from less common woods such as lilac, plum and honeysuckle, but has now converted to cherry wood because of its striking colour and grain, its durability and its smooth finish, all of which give the spoons a unique blend of balance and warmth.[12]

Beautiful wooden bowls are turned from black-cherry burls because of their unusual grain patterns. Burls are growths on a tree caused by an irritation in the growing tree from insects, stress, fungi, viruses and so on. The tree surrounds the irritation with rapid wild growth in order to isolate it, similar to a pearl growing in an oyster. The resulting grain patterns often present in such burls are highly prized by woodworkers. Also in the United States, beginning in the 1940s, Richard and Berdina Crowe of the Eastern band of Cherokee in North Carolina created handmade figurines from cherry wood, many of which are now in the Smithsonian National Museum of the American Indian. Richard was born into a family of Cherokee woodcarvers and designed and carved the doll figures from cherry wood. Berdina made authentic nineteenth-century clothes for the dolls that were typical of those worn by many southeastern tribes. Richard preferred to work with cherry because it 'has the color of an Indian's complexion and looks real when you sand it'.[13]

Traditionally, solid mountain cherry planks, called *moku hanga*, are used in Japanese printmaking. Making the woodblocks is an arduous process. The rough blocks first have to dry for four years, then need to be finished by joining small pieces to make larger blocks, reinforcing the ends of the blocks to prevent warping.[14] The blocks are then planed by hand. Today in Japan, the mountain cherry is rare, and only one or two artisans are left who know how to prepare the blocks for printmaking. Because of the scarcity of the mountain cherry, some printers reuse old blocks that have been planed down flat, while others have moved on to use different kinds of wood entirely. New England black cherry is commonly used as the veneer for these blocks since it is similar to the mountain cherry of Japan.

Another interesting use of cherry wood is for making musical instruments. While the wood itself does not add different tones to the music, it does absorb certain frequencies, affecting the final sound. The wood, frequently found in banjos, harps, mandolins and guitars, is prized for its beautiful colour and for its ability to be polished to a very high finish. Canadian Mark Saumier is a luthier who harvests local woods, including black cherry, to construct his instruments. In 2010 he conceived the Cherry Seven Project, in which he collaborated with musical instrument craftsmen. He invited the luthiers to build instruments using woods from the same trees, including black cherry, resulting in a collection of beautifully crafted handmade guitars that were featured at the Montreal Guitar Show that year.[15]

Because of its acoustic properties, American black cherry was used in the construction of the Kazakhstan Central Concert Hall

Cherry-wood harp,
Bucharest, Romania.

in Astana. Nicknamed 'Flower of the Steppes' and designed by the Italian architect Manfredi Nicoletti, the internal piazza of the building is clad entirely in American black cherry, which is also used in the suspended panelled ceiling of the auditorium.

In the lore of the Harry Potter series magic wands can be made of various materials and perform many supernatural functions. One wand manufacturer claims that 'cherry wands performs the most admirably in the following subjects: transfiguration, charms, divination, herbology, and astronomy.' This online Potter expert goes on to say that 'when performing magic this wand emits sparks of white and various pinks. A soft cherry blossom scent lingers around this wood.'[16]

In other magic belief systems, cherry wood is said to contain the element of earth energy: it is well grounded, solid and unwavering. Cherry wood, incense, stones and fruit are powerful aids for divination, medium works and healing. Cherry wands are a potent tool in fertility spells, and according to the website Wiccan Altar, cherry 'induces lust more than most other aphrodisiacs' and 'Enchanted Cherries are especially powerful in seduction spells.'[17]

Also magical is the traditional belief, in Wester Ross in the Scottish Highlands, that a cherry wood walking stick can prevent a walker from getting lost. The bark of the black cherry is rough on the main trunk of the tree, but the branches often have an interesting grey or even gold-like patina.[18]

There are several versions of the *Legend of Raueneck Castle* involving cherry wood, cherry stones, giants and ghosts. The version on the Storyfest website of Robert and Mary Wilhelm begins:

At the middle of his life's journey, the Knight of Raueneck Castle amassed a treasure trove of gold. So fearful was he that his gold would be stolen that he hired two giants to build a moat around his castle, and then a wall around his moat. His condition was that the wall be so perfect that not even a cherry pit should fit between any two stones in the wall.

The knight proved ungrateful to the giants and sent them away empty-handed.

One cursed, 'You will not enjoy your gold beyond tomorrow's sunrise.' The second added, 'And your ghost shall haunt your castle until a cherry stone is dropped from the beak of a raven – and falls into a crack between the fine and smooth, wall – which we built without even the blemish of a crack.'
And the first giant then rumbled, '. . . and until a cherry stone grows to be a great tree, and is chopped down, and is hewn into a cradle, for a newborn babe . . .'

The story winds on through episodes of ravens and cherry stones and a cherry cradle to an eventual happy ending.[19]

Because cherry wood is often associated with intuition, insight and overcoming obstacles such as writer's block, authors recording old folktales like the *Legend of Raueneck Castle* might very well use a pen made from cherry wood. Jim Cunningham, wood craftsman and founder of Heirloom Gift Pens, creates pens from fallen limbs of trees at historic sites in the U.S. For example, a cherry-wood pen has been made from wood present at the second battle of Trenton and another from the Battle of Brandywine, one of the longest battles of the American Revolution.[20]

It is not only the wood of the cherry that can be worked by craftsmen; the bark of the tree also has its place in arts and crafts. An interesting use for cherry tree bark has been the creation of Japanese cherry bark ware, known as *kabazaiku*, particularly in the production of Japanese tea caddies, or *chazutsu*.[21] About 220 years ago, low-level samurai began to make and sell tea caddies, as well as other cherry bark products, in order to earn extra income, and these continue to be highly desirable today. Other products included small cases called *inro* to hold medicine or tobacco, which were hung from strings on a man's belt and held in place by an anchor often carved of ivory, called *netsuke*.[22]

In this Japanese craft only the bark from wild cherry trees is used, because the bark of cultivated cherry trees is not sufficiently tough. In the spring scouts go up into the mountains where the wild trees grow and identify the cherry trees, easily spotted by their stunning pink blossoms. The bark is harvested after the rainy season in August or September, when it is softer and easier to remove from the tree. The bark removal does not damage the tree, as it will regenerate new bark. An additional layer can be removed from the second-growth bark. Interestingly the appearance will be quite different from that first layer of original bark. Kakunodate in Japan is the only place in the world where natural cherry bark ware is made; today there are just five companies still in the business.[23]

Ayers cherry pectoral syrup postcard advertisement, 19th century. On the back it boasts, 'Its powerful uniform control over all diseases of the throat and lungs makes it the most reliable medicine that can be procured.'

Native Americans had many uses for wild cherry trees, including medicinal preparations made from the bark of the chokecherry. The bark was used to relieve many ailments as described on the website the Herbal Academy, which cites information from Daniel Moerman's book *Native American Food Plants: An Ethnobotanical Dictionary*:

> The Cherokee used it for coughs, colds, fevers, indigestion, to ease labor pains, as a blood tonic, and as an astringent wash for sores and ulcers. The Chippewa use it to expel worms, disinfect and dress burns, cuts, wounds, and ulcers, and treat cholera and tuberculosis. The Delaware used it for diarrhea, coughs, and as a tonic for general debility. The Iroquois used it for coughs, colds, fevers, headaches, bronchitis, lung inflammation, sore throats, blood purification, sores caused by 'bad blood,' and burns. The Ojibwa used it for chest pain and soreness.[24]

Early colonists in the New World also used chokecherry bark as an ingredient in their cough preparations, no doubt having learned about it from the indigenous tribes. As a result of that contact, the

U.S. *Pharmacopeia* in 1820 added chokecherry bark as an antitussive and sedative.[25] Some of the symptoms said to be reduced by cherry bark were dyspepsia and other gastrointestinal illnesses, sore throats, pneumonia and irritability of the nervous system. The bark was used to give cough syrup a more palatable flavour. Cherry bark tea, medicinal in itself, was used to mask the taste of unpalatable medicines, and as a poultice or salve for abscesses, burns and ulcers.

Cherry bark was used in *kinnikinnick*, 'that which is mixed', a combination of various barks, grasses and herbs that served as 'tobacco' for Native American pipes. Indigenous people smoked pipes for social reasons, but also in healing ceremonies, so here too cherry bark could be considered medicinal. Herbalist Jim McDonald states, 'Tobacco's very essence is that of Prayer Medicine, and it is in this context that it can be used as a powerful ally and spiritual medicine.'[26]

Both cherry bark and cherry stems are used to create medicinal infusions.

Survivalists claim that eye soreness and snow-blindness can be treated by steaming inner bark and placing your face over the steam as an eyewash.

Once Native Americans peeled away the bark of cherry trees for its several uses, they discovered yet another versatile product from the tree: sap. Sap is mostly water with dissolved sugars and mineral salts that circulates in the vascular system of a plant. The sap of the

Sap oozing from a cherry tree on George Washington's Ferry Farm, Fredericksburg, Virginia.

cherry tree is a clear to amber gum that exudes from its bark during the tree's dormant season of November to March. If the sap appears cloudy in colour, containing dead tissue, the reason is likely to be a disease known as gummosis. Sap can also exude from bacterial cankers that can form on cherry trees.

According to some historians, Native Americans may have taught early American colonists how to use the residue of cherry tree sap as a chewing gum. The clear and tasteless sap dries to a chewy consistency, and is sugar-free.[27]

Native Americans also used the sap of the cherry tree as an adhesive. When heated and mixed with ash from animal fat, it produced a strong water-soluble glue, useful for attaching arrowheads to shafts and blades to knife handles. Mixing cherry sap with cereal crops made a thick and tasty gluey material that Native Americans spread on tree branches to entrap small birds. Native Americans of California used the sap from *Prunus ilicifolia*, also called hollyleaf cherry or islay, as a drink or sweetener.[28]

Medical uses were also found for the gum or sap of the cherry tree in Europe. Nicholas Culpeper in his 1653 book *Culpeper's Complete Herbal* wrote:

> The gum of the cherry-tree, dissolved in wine, is good for a cold, cough, and hoarseness of the throat; mendeth the colour in the face, sharpeneth the eyesight, provoketh appetite, and helpeth to break and expel the stone; the black cherries bruised with the stones, and dissolved, the water thereof is much used to break the stone, and to expel gravel and wind.[29]

Plant Lore, Legends and Lyrics, written in 1884 by Richard Folkard, suggests some amazing possibilities for the power of cherry sap. He cites a claim that 'during a siege, upwards of one hundred men were kept alive for nearly two months, without any other nutriment than that obtained by sucking this gum'.[30]

Although parts of the cherry tree have curative and medicinal properties, it also has a dark side. Simply put, the cherry tree is poisonous. Wild black cherry trees are a common fencerow and woodlot species in various parts of the U.S. Some animals, such as white-tailed deer, can safely browse on seedlings and saplings of the tree, despite the fact that cherry tree seeds, twigs, bark and leaves naturally contain a chemical called cyanogenic glycoside. The leaves normally have a bitter taste, which discourages horses and cattle in pastures from grazing on them. But if the trees are storm-damaged or knocked down by tornadoes, the leaves will wilt and, as they do so, their taste becomes less disagreeable. When livestock graze on the wilted leaves, the glycoside is hydrolysed in their bodies, creating a poisonous hydrogen cyanide toxin called prussic acid. University and government county extension services warn farmers to keep their livestock out of pastures that contain cherry trees with wilted leaves and, since tornadoes can carry broken branches great distances, also recommend farmers remove any cherry tree branches that may have been blown into their pastures.

An unusual case of livestock poisoning occurred in 2001 in the Lexington area, where thoroughbred racehorses were grazing on the famous Kentucky bluegrass. In the spring of that year, hundreds of mares either miscarried or delivered stillborn foals. Researchers at the University of Kentucky Agriculture Department traced the problem to Eastern tent caterpillars that had been feeding on black cherry tree leaves that contained higher than normal cyanide levels, due to some unusual weather patterns. The toxin was concentrated in the caterpillars' bodies and was excreted into the grass where the mares grazed.

Some varieties of chokecherries may be poisonous, and it is best to avoid ingesting their leaves or seeds. While the cherry laurel tree (*Prunus laurocerasus*) is an attractive evergreen shrub, ingesting the leaves and twigs should also be avoided. In both cases, an almond-like scent may be noticed, which is a characteristic of cyanide compounds.

Notably, a person consuming an average amount of cherries is unlikely ever to suffer cyanide poisoning. Yet for many years it was rumoured that the untimely death of U.S. President Zachary Taylor in 1850 may have been the result of cyanide poisoning after he ate a large quantity of cherries and washed them down with milk. While this rumour has since been discredited, the actual cause of his death is still debated.[31]

Obviously, given the millions of kilograms of cherries consumed yearly all around the world and the low number of subsequent poisonings, the risk of cyanide poisoning is low and would require ingesting unusually large quantities of cherries with their stones, and other parts of the tree.

Cherry tree leaves are readily identifiable. All cherry trees have a narrow, single-bladed leaf, with the margins exhibiting a series of serrations resembling miniature saw-blade teeth. Cherry leaves develop alternately along the branches rather than in pairs.[32]

Most cherry varieties have leaves that are longer than they are wide. The leaves of the black cherry, for example, average 5–15 centimetres (2–6 in.) in length, with widths of 2.5–4 centimetres (1–1½ in.). Colours of cherry foliage vary between the upper portion and its underside. For example, black cherry leaves have an upper surface that is shiny dark green, while the underside is a much lighter shade of green. In autumn, the leaves of most cherry species change to yellow and/or red.[33]

Cherry leaf spot is caused by the fungus *Blumeriella jaapii*. It can infect the leaves, stems and fruit of cherry trees. The leaves show spots, turn brown and develop holes. Older leaves will yellow and drop from the branches. Another fungal infection is verticillium wilt which causes the leaves to yellow, starting at the bottom of the tree and spreading upward. Twigs and branches will also be infected, eventually killing them.[34]

While cherries have certainly been well represented in art, cherry tree leaves have also been used in the making of art. Native Americans used the leaves of chokecherry to create a green dye to paint hides. In

Autumn cherry tree foliage, Cincinnati, Ohio.

Japan *washi* is an artisanal paper that can be made from a combination of cherry blossoms and autumn cherry leaves. Cherry blossoms and leaves are both important cultural icons in Japan; cherry leaves have often been depicted on *netsuke*.

Cherry leaves also play a small but important part in Japanese cuisine. *Sakuramochi* is a pink dessert, just like the cherry blossom flower, and is made from sweet, glutinous rice and filled with a sweet red-bean paste. The dessert is wrapped in a pickled *sakura* leaf that is also edible. A traditional time to serve this dessert is during *Hinamatsuri* (Girls' Day), which marks the beginning of spring and the cherry blossom season and is a time for wishing all little girls good luck and good health. The best-preserved leaves come from the Oshima-zakura variety of the cherry tree, which gourmets say has particularly juicy and fragrant foliage.[35]

Sakuramochi, Japanese sweet consisting of a pink-coloured rice cake and red bean paste centre wrapped in a pickled cherry leaf.

Ivory *netsuke* depicting a cherry leaf, Japan, 17th century.

Culinary uses of cherry tree leaves include tea and cherry leaf wine. Traditional recipes for pickling cucumbers include placing a cherry leaf in the jar, which will help keep the pickles crisp.

This chapter has highlighted parts of the cherry beyond the fruit itself that are not usually considered edible but have been used as medicinal and culinary elements in other cultures and earlier times. Researchers and foodies continue to experiment with new ways to use different ingredients, and all parts of the cherry have potential.

five
Literature, Legend and Lore

There is a garden in her face . . .
There cherries grow that none may buy
Til cherry ripe themselves will doe cry
THOMAS CAMPION[1]

Human beings are attracted to bright, shiny objects. Research show that we equate 'shiny' with 'pretty' – gold or diamonds, for example; but we also are drawn to objects that serve our innate needs. Studies suggest that 'shiny' reminds us of water. The colour red both warns and attracts us. Red cherry fruit against green leaves is a powerful complementary chromatic relationship. It is not surprising, then, that cherries, the shiniest, sweetest and brightest of red fruits, are irresistible to most of us.

In Chinese culture red is associated with joy, happiness and good luck. It is the colour of choice for traditional Chinese wedding dresses, and red clothing is worn during the celebration of Chinese New Year, when children receive red envelopes of money. Ripe red cherries are also considered a lucky gift, the red symbolizing prosperity and fortune, and the roundness of the fruit symbolizing perfection and eternity.

Humans are naturally attracted to sweet foods, a preference that begins with our first taste of breast milk. Sweets are the reward food of childhood, and, when the choice is fruit, cherries are among the sweetest of all.

Cherries are represented in every genre of painting, from still-life, landscape and portraiture to history and religious painting. It is a deliberate choice on the part of artists to paint cherries: their season is short and they are fragile. They are not an easy fruit to set up in a still-life or genre scene, yet their colour, shape and shine are alluring.

The earliest known cherry illustrations are found in classical Greek and Roman times, when artists delighted in portraying everyday objects such as flowers and food. One of the most unusual representations of food is in the collection of the Vatican Museums,

Giuseppe Arcimboldo, *Vertumnus*, c. 1590–91, oil on canvas.

Lips of Cherry,
Bright Eyes, Merry,
With a form divine;
Hear my heart sigh,
Tell me, may I
Be your Valentine?

where cherries – and even cherry stones, along with other food waste – are depicted on a mosaic tile floor fragment. The term for this clever variation of *trompe l'oeil* is *asarotos òikos*, or 'unswept floor'. The high status of the wealthy Roman host is brought home to his guests by the artistic rendering of remains of a luxurious meal.[2]

A Roman mural showing a sour cherry tree is preserved on the garden courtyard walls in the House of the Orchard at Pompeii, Italy, which was buried when Mount Vesuvius erupted in 79 CE. Birds, particularly parrots, and cherries were a popular subject in murals discovered in the ruins of Pompeii. A specific type of cherry known as 'bird cherry' continues to grow in that area.

During medieval and Renaissance times Christian symbolism developed into a complex language that assigned allegorical meaning

Wall-painting of birds and cherries, Pompeii, 1st century CE.

to many fruits and flowers, including the cherry, which many associated with femininity, fertility and the Virgin Mary. A cherry tree is listed among the trees and flowers planted in a nobleman's garden in the French allegorical love poem *Roman de la Rose* (The Story of the Rose). In an illustrated manuscript of that poem in the collection of the British Library, all the trees and flowers in the lush, walled space symbolic of the Garden of Paradise, including the cherry trees, miraculously come to fruit and blossom simultaneously.[3]

In the painting known as *The Garden of Paradise*, by an unknown Rhenish artist, the Virgin Mary sits in a garden paradise, safe from evil and corruption. She reads a prayer book as the baby Jesus plays nearby on a harp-like instrument. St Dorothy is picking cherries from a tree covered in fruit and placing them in a basket, which becomes an identifiable emblem of her sainthood. The basket refers to the miracle of fruit and flowers that appeared in her empty basket as she was martyred. The harvesting of the fruit could allude to the apocryphal story of the cherry tree bending down to allow Joseph to pick the fruit on the Holy Family's Flight into Egypt. It is possible that the twisted trunk of the cherry tree is meant to invoke an image of the serpent in the Garden of Eden.[4]

The symbolism and meaning of cherries in the iconography of Christian paintings, particularly of the Holy Family or the Madonna and Child, have been variously explained as representing the blood of Christ or referring to the Fruits of Paradise. The sweet red fruit

Upper-Rhenish Master, *The Garden of Paradise, c.* 1410–25, tempera on wood, showing St Dorothy picking cherries in the enclosed garden.

Frans Ykens, *Madonna and Child with Attendant Angels* in a floral cartouche with cherries, *c.* 1650, oil on panel.

Unicorn Tapestries: The Hunters Enter the Woods, c. 1495–1505, with cherry trees and fruit in the centre of the tapestry.

of the cherry symbolizes the sweetness of character that is the result of good works, or the delights of the blessed.

Set in an equally miraculous, lush environment, *The Hunt of the Unicorn* is a series of seven large tapestries woven around the year 1500. The action and images of the unicorn are modelled on a medieval stag hunt. They can be interpreted symbolically as a tale of lovers and a metaphor for the life and death of Christ, or as a meditation on the voyage of the soul in the afterlife. In any case, the cherry tree shown prominently in the first tapestry of the series stands as a symbol of both purity and innocence, as well as the fertility that all fruit represents.

Many of the wall tapestries from that time had fruit-and-flower garland borders, a motif derived from the Roman practice of draping garlands or swags of fruit and flowers on the sarcophagi of the deceased as part of the burial ritual. 'Garland paintings' became a specific genre in sixteenth-century Flanders, and cherries were often

Hieronymus Bosch, *Garden of Earthly Delights*, c. 1490–1510, oil on panel, detail of centre panel showing figures frolicking with cherries.

Jan van Eyck, *Arnolfini Portrait*, 1434, oil on panel. Cherries are just visible through the window behind the man, indicating summer.

included along with other fruits to create a motif of abundance. This was a bit of artistic licence since in real life the fruits would not have all ripened at the same time.

Cherries are a prominent motif in *The Garden of Earthly Delights*, a fascinating and mysterious work painted by Hieronymus Bosch

Detail of cherries from
Van Eyck's *Arnolfini Portrait*,
1434, oil on panel.

between 1490 and 1510. The central panel
of the triptych is the most difficult to explain,
as it is neither heaven nor hell. One curious
section of it depicts an owl perched on top
of an egg that covers two dancing figures
decorated with cherries. Equally curiously, a
cherry is being offered to a bird that balances
on a reclining human foot in the front right
corner of the panel. Though the interpretation of the symbols in the painting may have
been obvious to educated viewers of that
time, today there are many conflicting interpretations of Bosch's
symbolism, and very little agreement on what the painting actually
means. Art historian Peter Glum suggests, 'Four women carry cherry-
like fruits on their heads, perhaps a symbol of pride at the time, as
has been deduced from the contemporaneous saying: Don't eat cherries with great lords – they'll throw the pits in your face.'[5] Another
art historian, Michael Beyer, suggests, 'The voluptuous nude figures
can be interpreted as either portraying man in a primal state of nature
and peace, or the beauty and allure that the Devil uses to encourage
sin.'[6] Alternatively, the American writer Peter S. Beagle describes the
painting as an 'erotic derangement that turns us all into voyeurs, a
place filled with the intoxicating air of perfect liberty'.[7]

Cherries have been considered symbols of fertility and the sweetness of love, as represented in the 1434 *Arnolfini Portrait* by Jan van
Eyck. A tiny slice of the outside world showing a cherry tree in fruit
is barely visible through the window in the upper left, indicating the
summer season. Strangely, there is no known explanation of why
the couple is depicted richly dressed in heavy fur-trimmed winter
clothing.

While Van Eyck depicted the cherry tree in a secular, domestic
setting, many artists used the fruit image in a Christian context.
Cherries as Christian symbols, the Fruits of Paradise, the heavenly
reward for a virtuous life, may symbolize the purity and innocence

School of Leonardo da Vinci, *Virgin and the Child Holding a Branch of Cherries, c.* 1765, oil on canvas.

that prevailed in the Garden of Eden before man's temptation and sin. There are numerous paintings of the Madonna and Child, and the Holy Family, in which baby Jesus is holding cherries or cherries appear as a detail in the scene. A good example is the painting *Madonna and Child* from the workshop of Verrocchio painted around the year 1470 and now displayed at New York's Metropolitan Museum of Art.

One of the most famous depictions of this theme is *The Madonna of the Cherries*, painted by Titian in 1515. St Joseph is seen in the shadows on the left, and Zacharias, the father of John the Baptist, is on the right of the Madonna, while the child John presents cherries to the Madonna and baby Jesus.

Workshop of Andrea del Verrocchio, *Madonna and Child*, c. 1470, tempera on wood, with cherries symbolizing the blood of Christ.

Another sixteenth-century Flemish painter, or possibly a studio of painters, known as the Master of the Parrot, created works depicting the Madonna and Child with cherries as well as a parrot. A bird that miraculously takes on human characteristics of speech, the parrot is a metaphor for the essential Christian miracle of the virgin birth and appears in numerous examples of paintings of the Madonna and Child. From as far back as the early Roman wall paintings, the depiction of birds with cherries has been a symbolic combination favoured by artists.

Still-life painting in the western European tradition emerged from the symbolism of earlier Christian painting and developed into a complex visual language during medieval and Renaissance times. The realistic details in the religious paintings began to show up in contemporary surroundings, and eventually became the subjects of the painting themselves, with the religious narrative in the background. Joos van Cleve, in the early sixteenth century, painted several versions of the Holy Family, reflecting the growing trend of portraying

Titian, *Madonna of the Cherries, c.* 1515, oil on canvas.

Abraham Brueghel (1631–1697). *Still-life*, oil on canvas. The fruit and flowers include cherries.

the Madonna in an everyday environment. According to researchers at the Metropolitan Museum of Art, when an artist places fruit in a prominent place in the foreground of a domestic setting, he is referencing Christ's incarnation and sacrifice.[8]

Images of edible fruits, including cherries, are found in many genre paintings such as market and kitchen scenes, and can be appreciated on different levels by different audiences for their religious and secular symbolism, as well as their delightful, even astonishing, realism. The seventeenth century saw an explosion of interest in still-life paintings, particularly in the Netherlands. Dutch merchant ships returning from the Far East and East Indies trade centres brought back new plants, precious porcelain and rare trade goods. This new class of wealthy merchants became avid collectors and commissioners of art, including paintings depicting exotic plants and flowers from every season, sometimes unrealistically portrayed in a single bouquet. The price of a still-life painting for the patron would have been determined by its size and the number and type of details included, with cherries favoured for their attractive bright red colouring and shiny reflective surfaces.[9]

The Dutch enthusiasm for new optical devices such as the camera obscura, the telescope and the microscope also created a new demand and appreciation for scientific observation and illustration. New agricultural technology and horticultural innovations, including the use of fertilizers and irrigation systems, led to abundant food yields that were reflected in kitchen and market scenes.

While the Protestant Dutch were not interested in decorating their homes (or their churches) with religious scenes, one of the main themes of the Dutch masters was the idea of the 'vanity of vanities' or *vanitas*. The impermanence of all things and the proximity of death were the topics that most worried Protestant theologians in the opulent bourgeois society of that time. Cherries, with their short harvesting season and limited shelf life, represented, and continue to represent, a culinary luxury. The materialistic display of conspicuous consumption was both a matter of pride and a warning of the sin of culinary excess.

A subgenre of still-life, breakfast paintings illustrate simple fare typical of a Dutch meal. The food was often depicted on a table with a dark background and a monochromatic colour scheme. As with *vanitas* paintings, the intent was to remind viewers to follow moderation in all things, as in the consumption of cherries, which were certainly not among life's necessities.

Unlike contemporaries who painted beautiful portraits of upper-class ladies and children in their finest, Caravaggio, a seventeenth-century artist who often used fruit imagery, was particularly known for his paintings of everyday commoners who 'never washed their hands before eating'.[10] In *Boy Bitten by a Lizard*, a young man is reaching for sensual cherries with filthy fingers. Art critic Jonathan Jones writes, 'These cherries and all Caravaggio's fruits are not so much full meals as sex snacks.'[11] The young man recoils in pain and surprise as a small lizard he had not noticed in the pile of spoiled fruit nips his finger. Painted in typical Caravaggio style, emphasizing

Caravaggio, *Boy Bitten by a Lizard*, c. 1593, oil on canvas.

sharp contrasts of dark and light, the flowers and fruits are detailed and highly realistic, including both dark and light red cherries. Jones continues:

> The painting also contains complex sexual symbolism, which would have been quite clear to educated audiences in

Caravaggio's day: The bared shoulder and the rose behind the boy's ear indicate excessive vanity and a wish to be seen and admired, the cherries symbolize sexual lust, the third finger had the same meaning in the seventeenth century as it does today, and the lizard was a metaphor for the penis. The boy becomes aware, with a shock, of the pains of physical love.[12]

The fruit represents good and the lizard evil in Caravaggio's unique illustration of the battle between the two forces. Even darker and more frightening is Rembrandt's version of the *Rape of Ganymede*, a Greek myth painted for a Dutch Calvinist patron in 1635, in which a dark eagle violently carries away a plump cherubic baby who is gripping a bunch of cherries while crying and urinating in fright. Ganymede, who Homer tells us is the most beautiful of mortals, is abducted by Zeus, who appears here in the form of an eagle, to serve as a cup-bearer for the gods on Mount Olympus. While Rembrandt has chosen to represent Ganymede as an infant, he is most often portrayed as a beautiful young man. The myth suggests the Greek social practice of pederasty, described as an acceptable erotic relationship between an adult male and an adolescent male.

Art historian Margarita Russell suggests that in Rembrandt's time the bunch of cherries would have been recognized as a symbol of purity. 'Rembrandt must have seen examples of the motif; he probably knew the original or a copy of Titian's *Madonna of the Cherries*, which was once in the Netherlands.'[13]

Rembrandt's use of cherries is likely meant to be a substitute for the cup of nectar that Ganymede offered the gods of Olympus in other illustrations of this story. In a Christian interpretation of this pagan theme, the beautiful baby Ganymede represents the pure human soul who was presented as a symbolic gift to God. This was possibly a theme that would have comforted a family whose child was taken from them by death and is now represented as being with God.

Rembrandt, *Abduction of Ganymede*, 1635, oil on canvas. The terrified child
is clinging to a bunch of cherries.

Not as terrifying as Rembrandt's eagle and more reminiscent
of the Master of the Parrot are paintings that depict children feeding cherries to parrots or other exotic birds, which wealthy families
often kept as pets. Representing luxury and exotica at a time when
new worlds were under exploration, birds were also seen as symbols
of the soul and are a recurring theme of childhood innocence.

Christina Robertson, *Children with Parrot*, 1850, oil on canvas. Portraits of children and families with birds and cherries were a common theme among the wealthy in the 19th century.

The Scottish painter Christina Robertson (1796–1854) lived and worked in Russia and was commissioned by the Russian imperial family to paint numerous portraits, including several of their children, who always appeared sweet and virtuous. In one portrait, titled *Children with Parrot*, now in the Hermitage Museum, the cherry theme suggests the children's innocence. Many portraits of children include baskets of cherries.

In *The Cherry Pickers*, a work that was highly criticized yet very popular with his patrons, François Bouche portrays rural innocence with a hint of eroticism. The boy and girl in the painting are too stylishly overdressed for the job of harvesting cherries, indicating they are more at play than seriously working.

The painting *A Bearded Man and a Woman Feeding Cherries to a Parrot*, by the seventeenth-century Flemish artist Jacob Jordaens, shows an elegantly dressed young woman who could be assumed to be a 'kept woman' or high-class courtesan, a lovely creature who is 'caged' or kept as an exotic bird. The erotic symbolism of both cherries and the parrot kept as a pet would have been obvious to viewers of Jordaens' time.

Jacob Jordaens, *A Bearded Man and a Woman Feeding Cherries to a Parrot*, c. 1637–40, oil on canvas.

Nineteenth-century European Symbolist painters, such as Sir Lawrence Alma-Tadema, made extensive use of coded imagery in their work. The cherries offered by the temptress in Alma-Tadema's painting *Cherries* are more than a little suggestive, and clearly more than merely decorative. The painting was commissioned for a private men's club in Antwerp. Cercle Artistique was founded to promote the arts and sciences and to provide a congenial location where artists and their patrons could interact socially. The painting has been described as

> A daring composition executed in a bold style: an attractive woman gazes seductively at the viewer, as she holds out some cherries in an unmistakable gesture of sexual invitation. The erotically charged content and sketchy execution of the painting will undoubtedly have appealed to the sophisticated tastes of the connoisseurs who frequented the venue.[14]

In many paintings of women and cherries, the fruit functions as an accessory, a visually pleasing detail that supports and reinforces the painter's intent to illustrate the female subject of his painting as consumable, sweet, delicious and desirable. (After all, there are not many paintings of women and kale.) The vulnerability and danger to women who enhance themselves with too much paint or red lips, for example, is suggested by the saying dating to 1659: 'A woman and a cherry are painted for their own harm.'[15] Centuries earlier, the Japanese court writer Sei Shōnagon wrote in her series of lists in *The Pillow Book* in the year 1002, 'Things that lose by being painted: Pinks, cherry blossoms, men or women who are praised in romances as being beautiful.'[16]

Contemporary women have even bought into the complex and conflicting suggestions of the meaning of cherry as a metaphor. The American actress Halle Berry says, 'The man for me is the cherry on the pie. But I'm the pie and my pie is good all by itself – even if I don't have a cherry.'[17] Reality show star and pop culture icon

Lawrence Alma-Tadema, *Cherries*, 1873, oil on canvas.

Kim Kardashian was photographed erotically sucking a cherry in an October 2017 *Vogue* magazine photo shoot.

More sexuality is suggested in the still-life detail at the bottom left of Manet's famous and shocking 1863 painting *Le Déjeuner sur l'herbe* (Luncheon on the Grass). Many public parks in turn-of-the-century Paris were well known to be venues for prostitution, and the subjects here are clothed men and a naked woman accompanied by a sensual still-life with fruit, including a basket of cherries and a bottle of alcohol, both of which have spilled over.

Still-life painting played a small but significant role in the history of Impressionism and Post-Impressionism. Most of the artists of this movement painted cherries, attracted by their decorative form, rich red colour and the reflective quality of their shiny surfaces. In Renoir's portrait *Girl with White Hat and Cherries*, the vivid red of the cherries resembles the gentle blush in a child's cheeks, associating the figure with youthfulness and innocence.

Post-Impressionist Paul Cézanne was a slow-working, methodical painter who liked painting still-life compositions, particularly fruit, and spent considerable time arranging the individual fruits and groups of objects. His *Still-life with Cherries and Peaches* took more than two years to paint (1885 to 1887). It is reported that sometimes the fruit

Edouard Manet, *Luncheon on the Grass*, 1863, oil on canvas.

or flowers he used would wither and die before the painting was completed and would need to be replaced by paper flowers and artificial fruit. No doubt he had to replace the cherries more than once.[18]

In the twentieth century it would seem that Cubism would not be a style suited to painting cherries, but Pablo Picasso enjoyed painting the simplified, round shape and the bright spot of red colour that cherries provided for a number of his still-life compositions. Cherries even played a part in his personal romantic life. Françoise Gilot, in her account *Life after Picasso*, describes her famous meeting with the artist when he brought a bowl of cherries to her table at the Paris restaurant Le Catalan, where she was dining with friends. The gift of cherries was the start of a tempestuous relationship between the two; at the time, she was 21 and he was 61. She later left Picasso and became one of the few people ever to defy him.

Twentieth-century Surrealist painters like Salvador Dalí used images and motifs that had complex and personal meanings. Dalí used cherries in a number of his paintings, and gave a detailed explanation of his inclusion of a pile of cherries on the seat of a chair in *Six Apparitions of Lenin on a Piano*. The cherries here are a reference to the ones he painted on a door when he was a child, on to which he also glued real cherry stems, inventing what we would today call a mixed-media montage. His paintings often contain codes and subtleties that made sense only to the artist himself.

With the movement in mid-twentieth-century art towards abstraction and non-representational compositions, cherries as a subject came to have less allure. One exception might be *Little Cherry* by Hans Hofmann, rather sinister with its stained and painted blobs of reddish-brown tones, and open for sexual interpretation.

For Pop artists, though, such as Andy Warhol and Claes Oldenburg, the image of the cherry had immediate appeal. More universally recognizable even than a can of Campbell's soup, the colour and shape of a cherry are graphically appealing. In 1955, creating this popular and easily repeatable image of the cherry with the technique of stamping,

Paul Cézanne, *Still-life with Cherries and Peaches*, 1885–7, oil on canvas.

Amy Yosmali, *Cherry Bounce*, 2018, acrylic on canvas. Yosmali is a contemporary abstract artist inspired by the energy and symbolism of cherries.

Warhol designed a successful marketing campaign for I. Millar & Sons shoes, earning him the nickname 'the shoe person'.[19]

From Pop art to popular culture, the cherry remains a vivid motif that can range in meaning from modern sexual edginess to nostalgia for the innocent pleasure of childhood. Fashions featuring cherries and cherry blossoms are currently in style, from high-end handbags and shoes to children's dresses with cherry buttons. For more than fifty years these charming dresses have been sold, in a limited number each year, by the Woman's Exchange in St Louis, Missouri. The proceeds support not only the talented seamstresses who make a fair living wage fashioning the now trademarked dress, but refugee and immigrant training programmes in the area. Skyrocketing to fame when the little boy's version was photographed on John F. Kennedy Jr, the cherry dress continues to be a classic, recently purchased for their children by celebrities such as Gwyneth Paltrow.[20]

Cherries have also been popular in children's games. One of the highlights for children at any cherry festival is the cherry-stone-spitting competition. Hi Ho! Cherry-O, a children's board-game first produced in 1960, is a game in which players compete to collect ten cherries. It remains popular and can still be found in toy shops today. There are many cherry references in children's toys, especially for little girls, from Sakura Dolls to the Cherry Jubilee limited edition of My Little Pony.

Claes Oldenburg, *Spoonbridge with Cherry*, 1985–8, Minneapolis.

The cherry also features in adult games, notably in gambling slot machines, and even in modern digital and virtual games the nostalgia for the familiar winning symbol endures. The earliest slot machines, in the early twentieth century, used five symbols – diamonds, spades, hearts, horseshoes and the Liberty Bell – and were soon established in saloons and barbershops across the United States. Anti-gambling legislation went into effect about the same time, so in 1910 a new version of the machine was introduced and billed as a trade stimulator, a game of chance where people could win cigarettes, sweets or flavoured gum, thus avoiding anti-gambling rules. The playing-card-style symbols were replaced with symbols of the flavours of gum a player could win, such as cherry, orange, plum and lemon. This is why slot machines – especially in Britain, where they became popular in

Gucci cherry-embellished leather pumps, 2018.

Vintage Bakelite jewellery, 1920s.

the 1950s and '60s – are sometimes referred to as fruit machines, or fruities. David Sheldon, writing for casino.org, describes the nostalgic reaction to the fruit symbols:

> Whenever you see three melons or cherries, whoever you are, it triggers something inside you. Whether it's a nice memory from being a child, highlighting a sense of fun missing from today's cynical world, or just a reminder that gambling should be fun, fruit machines are designed to attract the punter in.[21]

Drawing on the nostalgia for the cherry and gambling connection, Cherry is the name of one of today's largest companies operating casinos and gaming activities. Founded in 1963 in Sweden, the company has developed a group that invests in and manages companies throughout the gaming industry, including online and virtual experiences.

Collectors of ephemera pay thousands of dollars for early twentieth-century products like tin trays or cherry syrup dispensers from the Zipp company's Cherri-O, whose logo is a robin sipping their cherry drink. Nostalgia for childhood flavours and experiences drives our desire for cherries and cherry-flavoured foods, from Cherry Coke to ice cream sundaes with a cherry on top. Cherry memorabilia is big business. For example, an original 1910 Zipp's Cherri-O soda fountain-top vintage syrup dispenser is valued at U.S.$2,000. Vintage cherry stoners can cost up to U.S.$300.

The cherry has made its way to television screens. In a famous scene in the hit show *Twin Peaks*, Audrey Horne slips a cherry between her bright red lips:

> Eating the flesh and tying the stem with her tongue, she embodied everything (resoundingly male) artists have thought about the cherry: She was overtly sexual but also innocent and pure. (And therefore, ripe for entering the infamous brothel, One-Eyed Jacks.) Fruit itself is innately sexual – after all, it is defined as the enlarged ovaries of flowering plants.[22]

Literature

Memories of the beauty of cherry blossoms in the spring, or the intense taste of the fruit, have inspired many poets to use cherry imagery, including Emily Dickinson, Robert Louis Stevenson, W. B. Yeats, Alfred, Lord Tennyson and A. E. Housman.

In her book *Shakespeare and Visual Culture*, Armelle Sabatier notes that 'In Renaissance love poetry, such as Spenser's *Epithalamion* (1594), the bright color of the cherry is conventionally used to describe a precise shade of red and as a metaphor to praise a lady's red lips.'[23] Shakespeare writes about the fruit itself or uses cherry imagery more than a dozen times and in several different ways, including with reference to the colour red and lips. In *A Midsummer's Night Dream* he writes 'O, how ripe in show / Thy lips, those kissing cherries, tempting grow.' He also uses the double cherry as a metaphor for a close relationship: 'So we grew together / Like to a double cherry, seeming parted, / But yet a union in partition.'[24]

In her article 'Forbidden Fruit: Why Cherries Are So Sexual', Amanda Arnold cites one of the most well-known early references to cherries and sexuality, found in 'There Is a Garden in Her Face' (1617) by Thomas Campion. Alluding to the call of seventeenth-century English cherry vendors, 'Cherry ripe!', Campion composed the lines,

> There is a garden in her face . . .
> There cherries grow which none may buy
> Till 'Cherry-ripe' themselves to cry.

He compares the fruit to a pure, virginal young woman who is forbidden to him.[25]

Jane Grigson writes, in her *Fruit Book*, about the seventeenth-century poet and priest Robert Herrick, who was known to have written poems to unattainable girls. A favourite 'prime of all' was Julia, the girl of cherry-time. He describes a day when he sat with Julia eating cherries and tossing the stones into a small hole, a country version of the English game quoits.[26]

Charles Cotton's *Erotopolis: The Present State of Bettyland* (1684) is an early example of seventeenth- and eighteenth-century English erotic fiction, known as Merryland, a pun on Maryland, that 'depicted the female body as a landscape that men explore, till and plow'.[27] Cotton compared the private parts of a prostitute to black cherries. The woman slowly reveals to the old man:

> A very fair Garden-plot of Maiden-hair, not green as in other Countries, but growing like a kind of black Fern, or rather a spot of Ground looking like a sieve of black Cherries, covered over with the tops of russet Fennel.[28]

In *A Dictionary of Sexual Language and Imagery in Shakespeare and Stuart Literature*, Gordon Williams traces the cherry's cultural influence back

Giovanni de Predis, *Girl with Cherries, c.* 1491–5, oil on panel.

to the sixteenth and seventeenth centuries, referring to some of the notable ways Europeans were using the fruit to talk about sins of the flesh.[29] Poets Josuah Sylvester and Robert Herrick liken 'cherrielets' to 'niplets' and 'teates' in multiple works. John Garfield refers to sex as 'playing at Bobb-Cherry' in the erotic pamphlet *Wandering Whore II* (1660).[30]

According to Jonathan Green, in *Green's Dictionary of Slang*, by the late nineteenth century the image of the cherry and its ripeness relating to virginity, and thus something that will eventually be lost, was well known. Green dates the origin of virgins 'losing' their cherry or getting it 'popped' or 'busted' to around the early 1900s. Depictions in the visual arts of young girls picking cherries or cradling baskets of them were common in those times.[31]

In *The Cherry Orchard*, the famous play by Anton Chekhov, written in 1903, the orchard plays quite a different role. Here it is portrayed as a relic of the past, a beautiful artefact, a luxurious, even wasteful, indulgence, with no practical function or value except as a reminder of another time now just a memory.

In his novel *Sons and Lovers*, D. H. Lawrence sets a playful and sensuous cherry-picking scene in an orchard:

> There was a great crop of cherries at the farm. The tree at the back of the house, very large and tall, hung thick with scarlet and crimson drops, under the dark leaves . . . the young man . . . tore off handful after handful of the sleek, cool fleshed fruit. Cherries touched his ears and his neck stretched forward, their chill finger-tips sending a flash down his blood. All shades of red, from golden vermilion to a rich crimson, glowed and met his eyes under a darkness of leaves.

Lawrence describes a similar sensuous scene in his poem 'Cherry Robbers':

> Against the haystack a girl stands laughing at me,
> Cherries hung round her ears.
> Offers me her scarlet fruit: I will see
> If she has any tears.

Less famous than the avant-garde writer Gertrude Stein's notorious pronouncement 'Rose is a rose is a rose is a rose' is her enigmatic line, 'Not a cherry a cherry not a cherry not a cherry a strawberry' from her opera *A Bouquet: Their Wills*, written in 1928. The 'Not a cherry' line evolved from her conversations with her Vietnamese chef, Trac:

> In his sweet-and-savory cooking, as in his Stein-like language. 'He would say, not a cherry, when he spoke of a strawberry,' 'and a pineapple was a pear not a pear'. Trac's inventive use of negatives slips directly into her prose.[32]

Folklore

American parents often teach their children the value of honesty through an apocryphal fable about George Washington concocted by Mason Locke Weems, an early Washington biographer, who included it in the fifth edition of his 1809 book *The Life of Washington*. In the story, intended by Weems to provide a morally instructive tale for youth, the young Washington supposedly chops down a cherry tree. When his father asks if he did the deed, he replies, 'I cannot tell a lie. I did cut it with my hatchet.' This story, though fictional, is a treasured part of American folklore and has been highly memorialized, including in a 1939 painting by Regionalist artist Grant Wood. Washington's birthday, 22 February, is celebrated with images of cherries and hatchets, and the gift shop in Washington's home at Mount Vernon stocks candy cherries and toy hatchets.

Over the years, many books written for children have included a cherry or cherry tree theme. Since 1923 Cicely Mary Barker's *Flower Fairies of the Trees* has enchanted young readers with its beautiful illustrations of flower fairies. Each illustration is accompanied by a charming poem that introduces children to the magic of flowers and fruit. The collection includes a Wild Cherry Blossom Fairy as well as a Cherry Tree Fairy.

Household Tales by the Brothers Grimm includes the tale of 'Cherry the Frog-bride'. With many variations, the story tells of a king who had three sons, all of whom fell in love with a beautiful maiden. She was named Cherry because she liked cherries better than any other kind of food, and would eat nothing else. In the course of many travails and encounters with an evil fairy, Cherry is turned into a frog, though eventually she is reunited with a prince.

A couple of newer children's books that contain a cherry theme are Vera B. Williams's *Cherries and Cherry Pits* (1986) and Alice Chandler's *Aunt Jane and the Missing Cherry Pie* (2017). Even *The Very Hungry Caterpillar* by Eric Carle has been eating cherry pie since 1969.

Some suggest the cherry symbolizes the womb, as it cradles the pits or cherry stones within the fruit. Pits have been used in fortune telling. One tradition suggests that to find out when you will be married, count out cherry stones, saying: 'This Time, Next Year, Sometime, Never'.

There is an old folk belief that one can discover how many years of life one has left by circling clockwise three times around a fruiting cherry tree on Midsummer's Eve, then shaking the tree very hard while reciting this charm:

Grant Wood, *Parson Weems's Fable*, 1939, oil on canvas.

> Cherry tree, I shaketh thee
> Cherry tree, pray tell thou me
> How many years am I to live
> By fallen fruit thy answer give.

Just as the last word is spoken, one should break away from the tree and then count the number of cherries that have fallen to the ground. This number is the age to which one will live.[33]

An English children's rhyme invokes the cuckoo to predict how many more years one will live. The rhyme says:

> *Cuckoo, cherry tree,*
> *Good bird tell me,*
> *How many years before I die . . .*

. . . with the answer being the next number of cuckoo calls the singer hears.

When using tarot cards to predict one's future, the card depicting the King of Pentacles, the Master of the World, is illustrated by a blossoming cherry tree, a white mountain and a large stately home. The cherry tree represents the natural resources available and financial wealth and prosperity, as finances can grow and blossom.[34]

According to Elune Blue, a website devoted to 'discovering magic and uncovering enchantment', cherries are associated with Venus, goddess of love. All foods, in Chinese herbal medicine theory, are categorized as either warm or cool. Cherry's characteristics as both warm (Yang) and sweet (Ying) suggest it can be considered an emblem of both femininity and kindness. 'The cherry is also associated with water and air, and connected to emotional, spiritual, and mental practices.' The site notes that 'cherry juice was even used to substitute for blood in rituals and magical workings because of its rich deep red color,' and suggests that specifically black cherries can strengthen psychic power and aid in divination. Their energy derives from the dual balance their properties represent, which is

Cherry fairy
postcard, German,
early 20th century.

necessary for achieving the much-desired goals of longevity and immortality.[35]

Cherries figure prominently in the folklore of many countries. Though more often described as a garden of peach trees, some versions of ancient Chinese lore describe the garden of the Goddess Xi Wang Mu as full of the cherries of immortality. 'Perhaps because of Goddess Xi Wang Mu, the Chinese consider cherries to be representative of femininity and beauty as well.'[36]

In both Danish and Swiss folklore an abundant crop of cherries was thought to be ensured by having the first ripe fruit eaten by a woman shortly after her first child was born. But not all cherry folklore has positive associations. Other European traditions hold that

CHERRY

certain forest demons hide in old cherry trees and bring harm to those who approach them. Kirnis is the Lithuanian demon who acts as the guardian of the cherry tree. In Advie in northeast Scotland it was considered taboo to cut the cherry tree, for it was regarded as a 'witch's tree'.

In Albania, according to De Gubernatis's 1879 *Mythologie des plantes*, old barren cherry trees were thought to be haunted by devils or demons. Anyone who might even accidentally find themselves under such a tree might be cursed with swollen hands and feet. Sicilian peasants living around Mount Etna hold a similar belief and would never choose to sleep under a barren cherry tree. St John's Eve was thought to be an especially dangerous time, when the Devil and evil forces were at work. Should a victim be cursed, the remedy was to cut a branch off the tree, symbolically 'bleeding the tree' and so removing the evil spell.

In Serbian mythology Vilas are fairy or elfin figures that dance around a wild cherry tree making sounds similar to those of a woodpecker. According to local lore, in a warning to stressed-out parents, if a mother sends her child 'to the devil' in anger, the Vila may seize the child. In the words of a Serbian ballad, translated by Bowring:

> Cherry! Dearest Cherry!
> Higher lift thy branches
> Under which the Vilas
> Dance their magic roundels.[37]

St Barbara was the beautiful daughter of a rich and powerful pagan named Dioscuro who grew up in Nikomedia (in modern Turkey). To safeguard Barbara's virginity while he was away, her father locked her in a tower. She converted to Christianity while he was gone, whereupon he denounced her, demanding that the local authorities put her to death. Barbara escaped from her tower, but was captured by her father and killed. At the very moment that he murdered her, he was struck by lightning. St Barbara is often depicted in art holding a small tower or standing near a tower. While imprisoned, she kept a branch from a cherry tree which she watered from her cup. Miraculously, on the day she was martyred, the cherry branch blossomed.[38]

Barbarazweig (Barbara's Branch) is the German custom of bringing cherry tree branches into the house on 4 December, hopefully to bloom on Christmas Day, a good sign for the future. Some reserve the custom for the unmarried and women who hope to have children. Because of St Barbara's association with protection from thunder, lightning and fires, she became the patron saint of artillerymen, as well as military engineers, gunsmiths, miners and all who work with cannon and explosives. She may also be venerated by anyone who faces the danger of sudden and violent death in their work. The Order of St Barbara is an honorary military society for artillerymen of the United States Army and Marine Corps.

Music

There are many songs that utilize the vivid imagery of cherries, focusing on their ephemeral quality of innocence, youth, beauty, ripeness, pleasure and life itself.

One of the earliest examples is the English Christmas song 'Cherry Tree Carol', dating back to the cycle of mystery plays around the year 1400 and performed in Coventry during the Feast of Corpus Christi. There are many versions, but it is thought that the story derives from the apocryphal Gospel of Pseudo-Matthew, which combines earlier Nativity traditions. Religious studies scholar Mary Joan Winn Leith connects the song to Crusaders in the Middle East. She writes:

> Around the fifth century . . . this storyline expanded into a full-fledged drama in the form of a Syrian Christian dialogue hymn sung in church by twin choirs – one singing the part of Joseph; the other, Mary – as part of the Christmas liturgy.[39]

The lyrics describe Joseph and the Virgin Mary walking through a cherry orchard. When Mary asks Joseph to pick her some delicious cherries, he refuses, saying that she should ask the one who 'brought thee with child' to pick the cherries for her. At that moment, as the song goes, the yet unborn Christ, performing his first miracle, speaks to the cherry trees from her womb, asking that they lower their branches so Mary can pick cherries. Joseph is astonished and immediately remorseful. The song has been recorded by many musicians, including Joan Baez, Judy Collins and Peter, Paul and Mary.

'The Riddle Song', originally titled 'I Gave My Love a Cherry', is a fifteenth-century lullaby. As with many traditional songs, the composer and date of composition are unknown. It has been recorded by many performers including Joan Baez, Sam Cooke, Burl Ives, Pete Seeger, Carly Simon and Doc Watson. By the twentieth century, there were suggestions that it contained hidden messages. The line 'I gave my love a cherry that has no stone' might refer to a woman who has lost her virginity. The line 'I gave my love a chicken that has no bone' might allude to pregnancy, as the 'chicken' referred to is a symbol for a baby inside the mother's womb.[40]

During the days of Allhallowtide, All Saints' Eve, singers go door to door, singing and saying prayers for the souls of the dead. In return, they are given soul cakes, containing dried fruit such as candied cherries. Celebrated in Britain and Ireland as early as the Middle Ages, the song 'A Soalin', also recorded by Peter, Paul and Mary, has a chorus featuring cherries with the following refrain.

> A soul! A soul! A soul-cake!
> Please good missus, a soul-cake!
> An apple, a pear, a plum, or a cherry,
> Any good thing to make us all merry.[41]

George Frideric Handel's pastoral 'Acis and Galetea', first performed in 1718, contains the aria 'O ruddier than the cherry'. Written as a form of courtly entertainment about the simplicity of rural life, some consider this one of the greatest pastoral operas ever composed. The cherry in the aria refers to the colour and sweetness of the nymph in this tragic love story:

> O ruddier than the cherry,
> O sweeter than the berry,
> O nymph more bright
> Than moonshine night.[42]

'Cherry Ripe' is an English song with words by poet Robert Herrick (1591–1674) and music by Charles Edward Horn (1786–1849). It contains the refrain:

> Cherry ripe, cherry ripe,
> Ripe I cry,
> Full and fair ones
> Come and buy.[43]

Julie Andrews sings 'Cherry Ripe' in the 1982 film *Victor/Victoria*. In the 1999 television adaptation *Alice in Wonderland*, Alice also sings it.

Perhaps the most well-known song featuring cherries was written by Lew Brown and Ray Henderson, who had a positive message about life during difficult times when they created 'Life Is Just a Bowl of Cherries', recorded in 1931 at the height of the Great Depression. The lyrics carry the message that the pleasure derived from a bowl of cherries only lasts for a moment in time and ought to be cherished.[44]

In 1969 Tommy James and the Shondells released 'Sweet Cherry Wine', an anti-Vietnam War song that expressed James's Christian beliefs. James explained in interviews that the sweet cherry wine is 'a metaphor for the blood of Jesus'.[45]

Clearly there is no better testament to the popularity and power of the cherry than its preponderance in so many forms of literature, legend and lore.

six

The Future of Cherries
ᖀᑌᕐᖇ

I s there an astounding tangerine-sized stoneless cherry or a
plate-sized eight-petal cherry blossom in our future? What
are professional researchers and pomologists looking for in
the fruit-bearing and flowering cherry cultivars in the years ahead?
Agricultural specialists and plant breeders working with the fruit-
bearing cherry tree are hoping to develop cultivars that address
several issues related to cherry production.

Researchers are seeking to develop cultivars that will allow for
an extended growing season, and cultivars that will bloom more than
once a year. Cultivars that demonstrate more winter hardiness, or
that bloom later when frost is no longer a risk factor, will also extend
the growing season and thus produce more cherries. Researchers are
also exploring ways to extend the range of cherry trees by developing
cultivars for certain microclimates that have not yet been suitable for
cherry growth, and also that do well in terraced orchards.

Increasing the precocity of trees means they will reach maturity
faster and produce a cash crop sooner. There is ongoing focus on the
development of more precocious cultivars and rootstocks. Currently,
cherries all around the world are predominantly propagated on only
two rootstocks, 'Mazzard' (*P. cerasus*) or 'Mahaleb' (*P. mahaleb*).

The development of cultivars that exhibit greater disease and pest
resistance is an important field of inquiry. Integrated pest management, including biological control agents, is increasingly being viewed
as an effective and environmentally friendly approach to disease

management; brown rot has been successfully treated this way instead of using chemical fungicides. Current research for bacterial canker involves inoculating young shoots with a pathogen and measuring the advancement of the disease through the tissue, thereby helping to identify cherry cultivars and breeding lines with resistance to bacterial canker. These natural methods may reduce or even eliminate the use of chemicals that are often hazardous to the environment. As an example, Amy Iezzoni at the University of Michigan has performed extensive research on cherries, particularly the eastern European cultivars she has collected. Her work has resulted in a new cultivar called 'Balaton', which was developed in 1998 and incorporates the robust genetic stock of eastern European varieties.

New cultivars are being developed that have greater tolerance for abiotic stressors such as winter injury, spring frost or heat stress. Cracking, caused by rain, is a common stressor that growers are trying to eliminate.

Mechanical harvesting requires the tree to be shaken so that cherries drop from its branches into a cushioned net. The shaking has to be vigorous enough to bring down the cherries but gentle

Michigan cherry varieties on display at the Northwest Michigan Horticultural Research Center, Traverse City.

enough not to damage the tree. Researchers are looking to develop cultivars that are more tolerant to shaking.

In addition to developing new cultivars, researchers and growers are continuing to explore ways to improve orchard management and harvesting techniques, and to extend the shelf life of cherries. New methods of orchard management include pruning systems, like the Upright Fruiting Offshoot (UFO) method, which allow branches to receive more light so the fruit can develop better, in addition to making harvesting easier. Improvements in rootstock have resulted in hardier dwarf trees from which it is easier to harvest the fruit. Polytunnels create microclimates that improve production and provide protection from birds. Improvements in transportation and storage help to reduce bruising of the fruit.

Much research has been directed at increasing the profitability of growing cherries. Research is also taking place to more accurately determine consumer taste preferences. The size of the fruit is an important factor. One researcher suggested 12 grams (less than half an ounce) as the ideal weight, not too big and not too small.

Cultivars that improve taste are being developed, and 'taste' does not simply mean sweetness. Scientific tools, such as refractometers and Brix level measurements, can measure the sugar-to-malic-acid ratio of the fruit. The proper balance between sweetness and tartness gives the cherry its characteristic taste. Researchers are working on cherry cultivars that have higher levels of antioxidants, nutrients and other compounds beneficial to health, without compromising on taste.

All this research and experimentation with cherry cultivars is resulting in a broader variety of cherries being offered in the market, similar to the many types of apples available to consumers. Germplasm repositories, fruit gardeners and fruit detectives (people who travel the world seeking out exotic fruits) are called upon to rediscover and preserve rare and heirloom varieties. It is important that researchers, farmers and producers inform the public of their new offerings. If informed consumers request specific varieties of cherries, then overall demand for them will be enhanced and expanded.

Consumers rarely put cherries on their shopping list; they are more often an impulse purchase. Cherry industry associations aim to increase the demand and create customers who specifically seek out cherries rather than buy them on impulse.

Breeding programmes play an important role in developing these new cherry varieties. Most commercially cultivated sweet cherries can be traced to their European origins. There are only four breeding programmes in North America, and almost all the varieties developed by them derived from only five founding cultivars. With the recent sequencing of the genome for the sweet cherry, we can expect that even more varieties will be developed.

Expanding the areas where cherries can be grown is important economically, especially in response to the ongoing impact of global climate change. For example, in the berry-growing regions of Scotland, raspberry crops in recent years have been ravaged by raspberry root rot, a disease that can infect whole rows of plants, causing them to wilt and die. Scottish growers are introducing cherry varieties that are thriving and are more economically profitable.[1]

Ever searching for the fantasy of the perfect-tasting cherry, that is also able to be efficiently planted, grown and harvested, Dr Bob Bors and his team of sour-cherry plant breeders at the University of Saskatchewan have recently developed what they have named the Romance Series. These six tart cherry varieties, with the delightful names 'Romeo', 'Juliet', 'Cupid', 'Valentine', 'Crimson Passion' and 'Carmine Jewel', were bred as dwarf trees, or shrubs, with the ability to thrive on the prairies. In the trials, tart, dark-fleshed cherries were intentionally selected for their health benefits, but it is the romantic name chosen for the group that triggers the imagination and nostalgia surrounding this much-adored fruit.

Developed at the University of New Hampshire, the Meader bush cherry (*P. japonica x P. jacquemontii*) cultivars, 'Jan', 'Joel' and 'Joy', are relatively easy to harvest, and ripen in late August and early September. They have the potential to extend the tart cherry season, but the berries have 'a distinctive flavor that is an acquired taste'.[2]

At the Research Station for Fruit Growing in Piteşti, Romania, new cherry cultivars with large fruit and good productivity have been obtained by mutating plant cells. This may occur spontaneously in nature or can also be achieved experimentally, using laboratory procedures. Romania maintains a collection of over six hundred genotypes of sweet and sour cherries.[3]

Under the auspices of the University of Reading and the UK Farm Advisory Team, the Brogdale National Fruit Collection, one of the largest fruit collections in the world, is an important source for research and breeding. In 1996, 285 varieties of cherries were replanted. One of the most important goals of the collection is the conservation of genetic diversity. Cryopreservation of the germplasm provides additional long-term security for the collection.

Research into the health benefits of cherries will continue, and this will probably result in increased demand and availability of cherry products. Health-conscious consumers want a reliable source of concentrated cherries, such as concentrated juice or dried cherries.

The future will see even more cherry tree diplomacy. More Sister Cities programmes will arise to foster international friendship and understanding by sharing the beauty and spreading appreciation of

Mechanical harvester.

Chef Jamie Simpson
of the Culinary
Vegetable Institute,
Reformed Cherry, 2018.

the cultural importance of the flowering cherry. Urban community gardening projects, such as the Philadelphia Orchard Project and the Pleasant Street Community Garden in Cincinnati, Ohio, and edible landscaping projects represent a growing trend that will continue for cherries and other fruits.

In Kent, England, one must wait on a list for a year or more to rent a cherry tree to harvest. The demand for cherry trees is likely to continue, along with the popularity of 'pick-your-own' options in cherry-growing regions everywhere. The rent-a-tree option reflects the farm-to-table movement, providing consumers access to the freshest possible cherries, in consideration of the fact that this fruit can be easily damaged in packing and shipping.

Freshly picked, unadorned cherries may be the ultimate cherry treat, and today's experimental chefs are always searching for new ways to use ingredients. Chef Jamie Simpson of the Culinary Vegetable Institute, culinary historian Charlotte Voisey and cocktail specialist Peter Vestinos teamed up to create a variety of manipulations of the fruit, including an unexpected cube-shaped reformed cherry, with more experiments to follow in their 'Eat Drink and Be Cherry' project.

While researchers work on all dimensions of the fruit-bearing cherry tree, others, particularly in Japan, continue to research and develop

Authors Kirker
and Newman
plant a cherry
tree in Romania
as a symbol of the
partnership between
St John's Unitarian
Universalist Church
in Cincinnati and the
Szentlaszlo Unitarian
Universalist Church,
Romania, 2017.

improved varieties of the flowering cherry. What are these plant breeders looking for?

In Washington, DC, at the U.S. National Arboretum (USNA), Dr Margaret Pooler, research leader of the Floral and Nursery Plants Research Unit, studies flowering cherry trees. She is working on the genetics, breeding and evaluation of species, as well as generating newer varieties of cherry trees that, among other things, are cold-resistant, produce bigger blooms and are disease-resistant. She describes her research as having biological, environmental and even diplomatic implications:

> Society will benefit from this research in several ways. By selecting for disease and pest tolerance, these new varieties will hopefully require less input of pesticides in production

and in the landscape. The use of underutilized species in our crosses will broaden the diversity of flowering cherries in the landscape and allow more choices in terms of plant size, habit, flowering time, etc. Plus it is hard to measure but easy to see (based on visits this week to the Tidal Basin) the effect that cherry blossoms in spring have on society.[4]

Faced with climatic changes, and the potential disappearance of the iconic cherry blossom, so important to Japanese culture, scientists in Japan have used ion beams to create genetic mutations resulting in a new breed of tree that blooms throughout the year.[5] While the end is not necessarily imminent, it is clear that, since 1990, temperatures have been rising noticeably and the number of cherry blossoms being produced has decreased, according to Dr Tomoko Abe, head of the Radiation Biology Team at the Japanese state-run RIKEN research institute. He notes that as Japan gets warmer, the number of hours of sufficiently low temperature to produce the optimal blossoms is falling below the necessary 8,000. The Nishina Otome flowering cherry, produced through a process of ion beaming at the Nishina Center for Accelerator-based Science, does not require a cold spell to trigger growth in the spring and will typically bloom twice a year, producing beautiful blossoms during all four seasons when indoors, and in both the spring and autumn when planted outdoors.

Given the goals noted here and in the mission of various research institutes, it is important to remember that the ephemeral beauty of the cherry is the essential characteristic that gives both fruit and blossom their unique value. But it is precisely this fragile quality that makes them vulnerable in contemporary times. In today's society of abundance, we have become accustomed to 'having it our way' when we want it, and as much as we want of it, for as long as we want it. No matter who you are, no matter how many resources or how much money you have, there are only a few months every year when you can eat fresh cherries; you cannot make a cherry tree bloom on command. Both the blossom and the fruit make us stop and take notice of what

Freshly picked cherries, Linvilla Orchards, Media, Philadelphia.

surrounds us, demanding attention each on their own terms and in their own time. Whether it is the stunningly beautiful floral explosion in the spring, or a brilliant red cherry on the top of a dessert, or the rare privilege of picking and eating fresh ripe cherries from a tree, the cherry, its blossom, its taste, and the nostalgia these images inspire, exist in our collective memory as sensual pleasure, and even romance. We do not get to experience these things every day, and maybe that rarity is the best and most important thing of all. Maybe we should be wary that a super-cherry might not really be 'super' after all!

Recipes

Cherry Brandy

(*Apicius Redivivus, The Cooks Oracle*, by Apicius, first century,
trans. William Kitchiner, 1817)

To a pound of ripe Morella cherries mashed well with your
hands, add a quart of brandy; let them steep for three days,
then press the liquor through a napkin; sweeten it with good
lump sugar, let it stand a week in a covered vessel, and then
bottle it.

Cherry Torte

(*The Neapolitan Recipe Collection: Cuoco Napoletano*, trans. and recipe adaptation by Terence Scully, University of Michigan Press, 2002)

Get red cherries of the darkest available, remove their pit
and grind them in a mortar; then get red roses and crush
them well – I mean, the petals alone – with a knife; get a
little new and old cheese with a reasonable amount of spices,
cinnamon and good ginger with a little pepper and sugar, and
mix everything together, adding in six eggs; make a pastry
crust for the pan with half a pound of butter and set it to
cook giving it a moderate fire; when it is cooked, put on sugar
and rosewater.

Modern Adaptation:

1 pound (500 g) cherries
1 pound (500 g) ricotta cheese
½ cup (125 g) sugar
3 eggs
½ tsp ginger
1 tsp cinnamon
1 tbsp dried rosebuds, crushed
1 pinch black pepper
1 tbsp rose water

Mash, but do not puree cherries (if canned cherries are used, drain them before and after grinding). Note that the flavor of the pie is altered drastically by using dried cherries, giving the finished product a much stronger 'raisin-spice' flavor. Mix ground cherries, ricotta, sugar, eggs, ginger, cinnamon, pepper and rose petals. Mix well and pour into unbaked piecrust. Cover with top crust and bake at 350°F (175°C) until top crust is golden brown. Just before serving, make a small hole in the top crust and pour in rosewater.

Squash Soup with Cherries

Explorers Meriwether Lewis and William Clark recorded in their journal a meal that was 'a Kettle of boild Simmins, beens, Corn & Choke Cherries'. (Recipe adaptation from Leandra Zim Holland in *Feasting and Fasting with Lewis and Clark* (Emigrant, MT, 2003))

2 cups (480 g) butternut, acorn or kabocha squash,
or pumpkin cut into 1-in. (2.5 cm) cubes
1 quart (1 litre) vegetable stock
1 cup (240 g) dried cherries, seeded (chokecherries, if you
can find them!)

1 cup (240 g) corn kernels
¾ cup (180 g) white beans – cooked, then measured
salt and pepper to taste

Simmer the squash or pumpkin cubes in stock for 20 minutes until tender. Add the corn and cherries; continue cooking for 10 minutes. Before serving, add the white beans and simmer.

Cherry Preserves

(Martha Washington, *Booke of Cookery and Booke of Sweetmeats*, 1749)

To Preserve Cheries: Take 2 pound of faire cherries & clip of the stalks in ye midst. Then wash them clean, but bruise them not. Then take 2 pounds of double refined sugur, & set it over ye fire with a quart of faire water in ye broadest preserving pan or silver basen as you can get. Let it seeth till it be some what thick, yn put in yr cherries, & let them boyle. Keepe allways scumming & turning them gently with a silver spoon till they be enough. When they are solid, you may glass them up & keep them all the year.

Cherries Jubilee

Building on Queen Victoria's love of cherries, Auguste Escoffier, in 1887, created Cherries Jubilee in honour of the queen's golden anniversary as monarch. Escoffier adapted the old French method of preserving fruit in sugar and brandy to make this dish. He published it in 1903 in his cookbook *Le Guide culinaire*. Originally, it did not include ice cream. Cherries Jubilee became widely popular in the 1950s and '60s, for home cooks' dinner parties.

There is no recipe, per se; simply caramelize butter and sugar in a pan, then add cherries. Flambé it with kirsch and/or brandy and pour it over ice cream. See YouTube video in the website section.

Clafouti

Created in Limousin in southern central France a few centuries ago, clafouti is traditionally made with unstoned, dark sweet cherries, which give the dish an almond flavour.

240 g (1 cup) sweet cherries with stones
1 egg, beaten
½ tsp vanilla
2 tbsp flour
3 tbsp sugar
⅓ cup (80 ml) milk

Mix the egg, vanilla, flour, sugar and milk together. Pour over cherries placed in a small casserole dish, or ramekins. Bake at 175°C (350°F) until set (similar to a custard consistency).

Meggy Leves, Hungarian Sour Cherry Soup

Combine:
1 jar (24.7 oz) morello cherries in light syrup
¼ cup (50 g) sugar
1 cup (240 g) water
1 bay leaf
1 star anise
⅛ tsp ground cloves
¼ tsp cinnamon
¼ tsp salt
⅛ tsp almond extract
¼ tsp vanilla
zest of 1 lemon, plus juice of 1 lemon

Simmer for 1 hour.

Blend:
1 egg yolk
½ cup (120 g) sour cream

Place a portion of the simmering cherry soup into a blender. Slowly add the egg yolk/sour cream mixture. Then pour into the soup. Simmer on low for 15 minutes.

Mrs Truman's Bing Cherry Mould (Salad)

(Bess Truman, U.S. First Lady, 1945–53; Recipe as archived at the University of Missouri Truman Library Collection, 1950s)

1 large can 'Bing' cherries
2 packages cream cheese
1 package cherry Jell-O
1 package lime Jell-O

Measure the juice from the cherries and add water to make two cups. Heat and dissolve cherry Jell-O in this. When partly set, add cherries.

Make lime Jell-O with water. When partly set, beat in cheese. Put cheese Jell-O in bottom of mould; let set; then put cherry mixture on top. Serve with mayonnaise.

Dr Venner's Cherry Bread Pudding

(Adapted from Edward A. Bunyard, *The Anatomy of Dessert* (New York, 1934))

'Cherries being boyled with butter, slices of bread and sugar.'
2 eggs, beaten
2 tbsp melted butter
1 cup (240 ml) whole milk

1 tbsp kirsch
½ tsp vanilla
¼ tsp almond extract
3 tbsp cherry jam or preserves
½ tsp cinnamon
1 cup (240 g) cherries
2 cups (480 g) stale bread, cut into 1-in. (2.5 cm) cubes

Mix all ingredients together, pour into a casserole dish, and refrigerate for 2 hours or overnight. Bake, covered for 1 hour at 350°F (175°C).

Italian Almond Cookies

This recipe uses mahlab, a spice derived from grinding the kernel from a particular species of cherry tree (*Prunus mahaleb*) that grows in the Middle East and Mediterranean region. It is available in ethnic grocery stores, but almond extract can be substituted.

2½ cups (360 g) blanched almond flour
⅔ cup (130 g) sugar
½ tbsp ground mahalab (or almond extract)
½ tsp salt
4 egg whites
½ tsp vanilla
40 Amarena cherries

Combine the almond flour, half of the sugar, the mahlab and salt. Beat the egg whites to a stiff peak with the other half of the sugar and the vanilla. Fold the dry ingredient mixture into the beaten egg white mixture. Fill a pastry bag and press out star-shaped cookies. Place a cherry on top of each cookie. Bake 20 minutes at 325°F (160°C). Makes 40 cookies.

Albaloo polo, Persian Rice

(Adapted from *The Silk Road Gourmet* by Laura Kelley, 2009)

2 tbsp butter
1 large onion, peeled, diced and separated into crescents
1 tsp Advieh
½ tsp salt
¼ tsp black pepper
1½ cups (360 g) sour cherries in light syrup
2 cups (480 g) water
1 cup (175 g) uncooked basmati rice

Sauté the onion in butter. Add spices, cherries and water. Bring to boil and add the rice. For garnish, sprinkle with slivered almonds and pistachios.

Cherry Pie

Can she bake a cherry pie, Billy Boy, Billy Boy . . .

FOLK SONG

Of course she can. It is incredibly easy!

Providing a 'recipe' is almost insulting. The recipe from Comstock's canned cherry pie filling is only two steps. The recipe reads: pour the contents into the piecrust and spread it out.

If you wish to make your cherry pie from scratch, there are just a few variables to consider:

Cherries – A traditional cherry pie is made with sour cherries (fresh, frozen or canned, in that order of preference). Most often these are Montmorency cherries in the United States, but European varieties of sour cherries, such as morello, can be found in jars in the U.S. and used for cherry pie. Some bakers say the best pies are made with cherries picked within 24 hours of baking the pie. But, seriously, who can do that! A few recipes call for sweet cherries (usually Bing cherries, but can include Rainier or other varieties). Be sure to use stoned cherries in any case. In Europe a cherry clafoutis (a custard type of cherry pie) is made with cherries with their stones, which adds an almond flavour to the dish. In any case, you will need about 5½ cups (770 g) of cherries.

Sweetener – Depending on the sweetness of your cherries and your personal preference, you will need approximately 1 cup (200 g) of sugar. A few recipes note that a quarter of this sugar could be brown sugar.

Thickener – Use approximately 2 tablespoons of a thickener. The most common thickeners are flour, cornflour (cornstarch) or tapioca. Bakers disagree as to what is best, so it's mostly a personal preference.

That is it – cherries, sugar and thickener. However, bakers are always trying to make their pie stand out, so here are some additional flavour enhancers that have been used: vanilla, almond extract, kirsch, orange liqueur, lemon juice, lemon zest, cinnamon, cardamom and nutmeg.

Timeline

5000 to 4000 BCE	Cherry stones found in Stone Age caves, indicating that prehistoric people consumed cherries
300 BCE	Theophrastus mentions cherry trees in his *History of Plants*
70 BCE	Sour cherries introduced to the Romans by Lucius Lucullus
100 CE	Pliny the Elder's *Naturalis historia* mentions various methods of grafting cherries
100	Cherries arrive in Kent, England, with the Romans
710–94	Ritual cherry blossom viewing, *hanami*, begins in Japan and trees are transplanted in towns
1066	Norman conquest reintroduces cherries to England
1192	Samurai class rises to political power in Japan, and cherry blossoms exemplify the noble character of the 'Japanese soul'
1364	Charles V, king of France, plants 1,125 cherry trees in gardens at Tournelles and St Paul
1400s	*Tacuinum sanitatis*, the medieval health handbook, describes the health benefits of cherries
1415	The poet John Lydgate writes about cherries for sale in London market

1533	Richard Harris, horticulturalist to King Henry VIII, plants a mother nursery in Teynham, for distribution to other tree growers
1595	The *Gerard Herbal* is published, describing English cherries
1600s	Cherries come to America, brought by European settlers
1600s–1700s	Extensive planting of cherry gardens in Faversham Fruit Belt and Medway Valley in England
1611	John Tradescant the Elder introduces the 'Tradescant' cherry to Hatfield House, England
1648	The poet Robert Herrick writes 'Cherry Ripe', the lyrics of which are popularized in the folk song
1649	Two hundred trees in gardens of Henrietta Maria, queen of Charles I, at Wimbledon, England
1655	Duke cherries, a cross between sweet and sour cherries, are mentioned by horticulturalist John Rea
1669	Law passed for the preservation of all cherry trees in the royal forests of England
1755	Launch of the famous Portuguese Ginja liqueur by Lisbon shops selling sour cherries in *aguardente* (alcoholic beverage)
1773	William Bartram notes *Prunus padus* growing near Augusta, Georgia, in his book *Travels*
1800s	Cherries are introduced to Australia in the late nineteenth century
1811	Thomas Jefferson's records indicate his orchard contains 48 cherry trees
1815	The 'Waterloo' cherry is named after the battle of Waterloo

1847	Henderson Lewelling plants an orchard in western Oregon, thus beginning the Northwest sweet cherry commercial production
1850	U.S. President Zachary Taylor dies, with much speculation about the cause of death being from eating a large quantity of cherries
1860	Robert Hogg's *Fruit Manual* gives a comprehensive description of fruit varieties including cherry
1868–1912	Meiji Restoration promotes imperial nationalism. Cherry trees reflect the sacrifice of Japanese soldiers in service to the state of Japan. Emiko Ohnuki-Tierney writes that these soldiers were told, 'You shall die like beautiful falling cherry petals for the emperor.'
1875	Sweet cherry cultivar 'Bing' is developed by Seth Lewelling in Oregon
1879	Sir John Everett Millais paints *Cherry Ripe*
1880s	Grants Morello Cherry Brandy factory is built in Lenham, England
1892	First accounts of a 'Cherry Sundae' in Ithaca, New York: cherry syrup poured over vanilla ice cream with a candied cherry on top
1893	Sour cherry commercial production begins in Michigan
1896	Experiments in the U.S. to produce a version of maraschino cherries that uses U.S. varieties and less (eventually no) alcohol than the European versions
1902–3	Dr David Fairchild, at the U.S. Department of Agriculture, introduces thirty named varieties of cherry tree into the U.S.
1904	Debut of the *Cherry Orchard* on 17 January at the Moscow Arts Theatre on Chekhov's birthday
1910	Traverse City, Michigan, begins its cherry festival, 'Blessings of the Blossom', which later evolves into the National Cherry Festival

1912	Japan gives the U.S. 3,000 cherry trees to plant in Washington, DC
1921	The National Fruit Collection established at Wisley, England, by the Royal Horticultural Society
1926	To celebrate the 150th anniversary of American Independence, cherry trees are planted in Philadelphia, PA
1939–45	During the Second World War, in its colonial enterprises, imperial Japan plants cherry trees as a way of 'claiming occupied territory as Japanese space'
1940	The breeding of self-fertile cherries begins in British Columbia
1952–4	England's National Fruit Collection relocates to Brogdale Farm, Kent
1958	'Colt', the dwarf cherry rootstock, is bred
1965	Japanese government gifts Lady Bird Johnson 3,800 Yoshino trees (an ancient variety of cherry tree) that are planted in Washington, DC
1970s	In Beijing, Yuyuatan Park is home to more than 2,000 cherry trees, two hundred of them given to China by Japan in the early 1970s on re-establishing diplomatic ties
1981	Archaeologists at Thomas Jefferson's Monticello find four bottles filled with preserved cherries in the kitchen yard dry-well
1987	World's largest cherry pie at 5.3 m (17 ft 6 in.) at the National Cherry Festival in Traverse City, MI
2008	National Cherry Day is established in Britain as third Saturday in July
2009	Cherry Aid Project launches in Britain
2012	Release of the documentary film *The Tsunami and the Cherry Blossom*, in which a Japanese man reflects on the strength of cherry trees to live on past the devastation

References

Introduction

1 Pablo Neruda, 'Every Day You Play', in *Twenty Love Poems and a Song of Despair*, trans. W. S. Merwin (New York, 2006), p. 53.

1 History, Cultivation and Consumption

1 Marjorie Adams, 'Wax Fruit and Vegetable Model Collections', www.ecommons.cornell.edu, accessed 12 December 2018.
2 R. Watkins, 'Cherry, Plum, Peach, Apricot and Almond', *Evolution of Crop Plants*, ed. N. W. Simmonds (New York, 1976), p. 245; A. D. Webster, The Taxonomic Classification of Sweet and Sour Cherries and a Brief History of Their Cultivation', *Cherries: Crop Physiology, Production and Uses*, ed. A. D. Webster and N. E. Looney (Wallingford, 1996), pp. 3–23.
3 A. De Candolle, *Origin of Cultivated Plants* (New York, 1886), p. 176.
4 E. J. Olden and N. Nybom, 'On the Origin of *Prunus cerasus* L.', *Hereditas*, LIX (1968), pp. 327–45; Jules Janick, *Origin and Dissemination of Prunus Crops* (Hoboken, NJ, 2011), p. 56.
5 Don R. Brothwell, *Food in Antiquity: A Survey of the Diet of Early Peoples* (Baltimore, MD, 1997), p. 136.
6 Ibid.
7 W. Rhind, *A History of the Vegetable Kingdom* (Oxford, 1841), p. 334.
8 Anna Louise Taylor, 'British Cherries Make a Comeback', www.bbc.co.uk, August 2013, accessed 12 December 2018.
9 Will Bashor, *Marie Antoinette's Head: The Royal Hairdresser, the Queen, and the Revolution* (Lanham, MD, 2013), p. 65.
10 Mumtaz Ahmad Numani, 'Emperor Jahangir's Method of Observation and Approaches to Investigation of Kashmir Ecology: An Appraisal of His Deep Sense of Sensitivity towards Nature', *Journal of Ecology and the Natural Environment*, VII/3 (2015), p. 79.
11 'Thomas Jefferson's Monticello, "Carnation" Cherry', www.monticello. org, accessed 12 December 2018.
12 Jules Janick, 'The Origins of Fruits, Fruit Growing and Fruit Breeding', *Plant Breeding Review*, XXV (2005), p. 26.

13 Maria Luisa Badenes, *Fruit Breeding* (Berlin, 2012), pp. 459–504.
14 Dan Charles, 'Inside a Tart Cherry Revival: "Somebody Needs to Do This!"' www.npr.org, 23 May 2013, accessed 12 December 2018.
15 U. P. Hedrick, *Cyclopedia of Hardy Fruits* (New York, 1922), p. 136.
16 Janick, *Origin and Dissemination of Prunus Crops*, p. 83.
17 'The Story of the Famous Bing Cherry', www.cherries.global, accessed 26 December 2018.
18 Bryan Newman, 'Montmorency Cherries on French Menus', https://behind-the-french-menu.blogspot.com, 2017.
19 Ibid.
20 '*Ferrovia*', www.goodfruitguide.co.uk, accessed 12 December 2018.
21 Lynn E. Long et al., 'Sweet Cherry Rootstocks', https://extension.oregonstate.edu, February 2014.
22 Badenes, *Fruit Breeding*, pp. 459–504.
23 Virginia Cooperative Extension, 'Growing Cherries in Virginia', https://ext.vt.edu, accessed 27 December 2018.
24 Badenes, *Fruit Breeding*, pp. 459–504.
25 Michigan State University, 'History of Tart Cherries', www.canr.msu.edu, accessed 26 December 2018.
26 Long et al., 'Sweet Cherry Rootstocks'.
27 Virginia Cooperative Extension, 'Growing Cherries in Virginia'.
28 Keith Clay, 'American Black Cherry Tree Overruns Europe by Playing Dirty', www.newsinfo.iu.edu, 9 December 2003.
29 Wybe Kuitert, *Japanese Flowering Cherries* (Portland, OR, 1999), p. 189.
30 Ibid., p. 181.
31 Live Japan, 'The Five Great Sakura Trees of Japan', www.livejapan.com, 31 May 2017.
32 Ibid.
33 Michigan Farmer, 'Michigan Cherry Production Down from Previous Year', www.farmprogress.com, 14 August 2017.
34 James L. Wescoat, *Mughal Gardens: Sources, Places, Representations, and Prospects* (Washington, DC, 1996), p 129.
35 Geoff Herbert, 'Tree of 40 Fruits', www.syracuse.com, 8 August 2015.
36 K. W. Mudge, J. Janick, S. Scofield and E. E. Goldschmidt, 'A History of Grafting', *Horticultural Reviews*, XXXV (2009), p. 456.
37 Nikki Rothwell, 'Cherry Fruit Fly Ecology and Management', www.canr.msu.edu, 6 June 2006.
38 Luana dos Santos, 'Global Potential Distribution of *Drosophila suzukii*', www.journals.plos.org, 21 March 2017.
39 Ashley Welch, 'New Fruit Tops Dirty Dozen List of Most Contaminated Produce', www.cbsnews.com, 12 April 2016.
40 Joseph Addison, *The Works of Joseph Addison: The Spectator* (London, 1891), p. 463.
41 Jules Janick, *Origin and Dissemination of Prunus Crops* (Hoboken, NJ, 2011), p. 56.
42 'Where Do Cherries Grow? The World Leaders in Cherry Production', www.worldatlas.com, accessed 26 December 2018.

43 Adam Leith Gollner, *The Fruit Hunters: A Story of Nature, Adventure, Commerce and Obsession* (New York, 2008), p. 48.
44 Ibid.
45 Horticulture and Landscape Architecture, Purdue University, 'Tacuinum Sanitatis', www.hort.purdue.edu, accessed 27 December 2018.
46 Maguelonne Toussaint-Samat, *A History of Food* (Hoboken, NJ, 2009), p. 585.
47 Ewa Hudson, 'Cherries: More Than Just Antioxidants', www. euromonitor.com, 2012.
48 G. Howatson et al., 'Effect of Tart Cherry Juice (*Prunus cerasus*) on Melatonin Levels and Enhanced Sleep Quality', *European Journal of Nutrition*, LI/8 (2012), pp. 909–16.
49 Healthline, 'About Cherry Allergies', www.healthline.com, accessed 12 December 2018.
50 Susan McQuillan, 'Happiness Is (Literally) a Bowl of Cherries', www. psychologytoday.com, 5 September 2016.

2 Blossoms: Aesthetics of the Ephemeral

1 Kathryn Lasky, *The Royal Diaries: Marie Antonoinette, Princess of Versailles, Austria-France* (New York, 2000), p. 37.
2 Jules Janick, 'Origin and Dissemination of Cherry', *Horticultural Review*, LV (2010), p. 271.
3 Adrian Higgins, 'Beyond Washington's Cherry Trees, How Did so Many Japanese Plants Find Their Way into American Gardens?', *Washington Post Magazine* (23 March 2012).
4 Naoko Abe, *'Cherry' Ingram: The Englishman Who Saved Japan's Blossoms* (London, 2019), p. 195.
5 Ibid.
6 'Jefferson: The Scientist and Gardener', www.monticello.org, accessed 27 December 2018.
7 Basil Montagu, *The Works of Francis Bacon, Lord Chancellor of England* (Philadelphia, PA, 1852), p. 73.
8 Kendra Wilson, 'A Gothic Garden Visit, Courtesy of the Mitfords', www.gardenista.com, 27 October 2013.
9 Emiko Ohnuki-Tierney, *Kamikaze, Cherry Blossoms and Nationalisms: The Militarization of Aesthetics in Japanese History* (Chicago, IL, 2006), p. 27.
10 Michael Hoffman, 'Sakura: Soul of Japan', www.japantimes.co.jp, 25 March 2012.
11 Mark Cartwright, 'Ninigi,' www.ancient.eu, 4 May 2017.
12 Hugo Kempeneer, 'Hirano Jinja: Emperor Kazan's Favorite Cherry Tree Garden!', www.kyotodreamtrips.com, 17 January 2012.
13 'Yoshitoshi Tsukioka: Spirit of the Komachi Cherry Tree: New Forms of Thirty-six Ghosts, 1889–1892', www.sinister-designs.com, accessed 24 April 2019.
14 Joseph Castro, 'What's the Cultural Significance of Cherry Blossoms?', www.livescience.com, 4 April 2013.

15 John Dougill, 'Gion Festival: Chigo', www.greenshinto.com, 11 July 2013.
16 Mislav Popovic, 'Gion Matsuri', www.traditionscustoms.com, accessed 27 December 2018.
17 'Cherry Blossom Festival: Types of Trees', www.nps.gov, accessed 24 April 2019.
18 Emiko Ohnuki-Tierney, *Kamikaze, Cherry Blossoms, and Nationalisms: The Militarization of Aesthetics in Japanese History* (Chicago, IL, 2002), p. 97.
19 Emiko Ohnuki-Tierney, *Kamikaze Diaries: Reflections of Japanese Student Soldiers* (Chicago, IL, 2007), p. 28.
20 Merrily Baird, *Symbols of Japan: Thematic Motifs in Art and Design* (New York, 2001), pp. 48–9.
21 Jennifer Weiss, 'Cherry Blossoms in Literature and Art', www.tokyocreative.com, accessed 27 December 2018.
22 Ibid.
23 'Viewing Cherry Blossoms', www.blogs.loc.gov, March 2016.
24 Robin D. Gill, *Cherry Blossom Epiphany* (Key Biscayne, FL, 2006).
25 Yoshida Kenko, *Tsurezuregusa (Essays in Idleness)*, trans. Donald Keene (New York, 1998), p. 118.
26 Library of Congress Exhibit, *Sakura: Cherry Blossoms as Living Symbols of Friendship*, www.loc.gov, accessed 27 December 2018.
27 'How to Play Hanafuda Hawaii Style', www.hanafudahawaii.com, accessed 27 December 2018.
28 'An Intro to Karuta', www.japansocietyboston.org, 1 August 2017.
29 Julian Ryall, 'Japan Plants Cherry Trees as Guard against Future Tsunami', www.telegraph.co.uk, 7 November 2011.
30 Lucy Walker, 'The Tsunami and the Cherry Blossom', www.lucywalkerfilm.com, accessed 27 December 2018.
31 Anthony Kuhn, 'Celebrating Rebirth amid Devastation in Tokyo', www.npr.org, 4 April 2011.
32 Eliza Ruhamah Scidmore, 'The Cherry Blossoms of Japan', *The Century Illustrated Monthly Magazine*, LXXIX/5 (1910), p. 648.
33 'History of the Cherry Blossom Trees and Festival', www.nationalcherryblossomfestival.org, accessed 27 December 2018.
34 JoAnn Garcia, 'The Cherry Tree Rebellion', www.nps.gov, 15 March 2012.
35 'Roland Maurice Jefferson Collection', https://specialcollections.nal.usda.gov, accessed 27 December 2018.
36 'United States Japan Cooperative Initiatives,' https://obamawhitehouse.archives.gov, 30 April 2012.
37 Chloe Pantazi, 'An Unassuming City in Georgia Is the Best Place in the World to See Cherry Blossoms', www.businessinsider.com, 20 March 2017.
38 'Check Out Real Cherry Blossoms, Lifelike Dolls and More at Gardens by the Bay', www.sg.asia-city.com, 19 March 2018.
39 'China, Korea, Japan in Cherry Trifle', www.thestar.com, 30 March 2015.
40 Elizabeth B. Moynihan, *Paradise as a Garden in Persia and Mughal India* (New York, 1979), p. 122.

41 Aisha Stacey, 'Treating Guests Islamic Way', www.islamreligion.com, 25 August 2014.

42 D. Fairchild Ruggles, *Islamic Gardens and Landscapes* (Philadelphia, PA, 2008).

43 C. M. Villiers-Stuart, *Gardens of the Great Mughals* (London, 2008), pp. 162–6.

44 Andrea Wulf, *Founding Gardeners* (New York, 2012), p. 39.

45 Quoted in William Alvis Brogden, *Ichnographia Rustica: Stephen Switzer and the Designed Landscape* (New York, 2017), p. 19.

46 'The Four Gardens at Mount Vernon', www.mountvernon.org, accessed 27 December 2017.

47 Ibid.

48 Susan P. Schoelwer, *The General and the Garden* (Mount Vernon, VA, 2014), p. 114.

49 'The Four Gardens at Mount Vernon'.

50 Élisabeth de Feydeau, *From Marie Antoinette's Garden: An Eighteenth-century Horticultural Album* (Paris, 2017).

51 'Sakura Folk Song', www.self.gutenberg.org, accessed 27 December 2018.

52 'It Looks Like Rain in Cherry Blossom Lane', www.archive.org, accessed 27 December 2018.

53 'Revolutionary Song in France', www.libcom.org, 11 September 2006.

54 'How Nomaterra Whipped up Their Cherry Blossom Fragrance', www.dc.racked.com, 27 March 2014.

55 Kyril Zinovieff and April Fitslyon, trans., *Three Novellas by Leo Tolstoy, Family Happiness* (London, 2018), p. 193.

3 Fruit: From Tree to Table

1 Edward Bunyard, *The Anatomy of Dessert* (New York, 1934), p. 50.

2 Ibid., p. 49.

3 Gina Marzolo, 'Cherries', www.agmrc.org, 2015., accessed 12 December 2018.

4 'Monts de Venasque Cherry', www.ventoux-sud.com, accessed 19 April 2019.

5 'Chinese Demand Propels Chile's Fruit Exports to Record High', www.xinhuanet.com, 9 November 2018.

6 Gillian Rhys, 'Who Invented the Singapore Sling?', *South China Morning Post* (6 August 2015), www.scmp.com.

7 'History Lesson: The Maraschina Cherry', *Imbibe Magazine* (19 December 2016), www.imbibemagazine.com.

8 Leandra Zim Holland, *Feasting and Fasting with Lewis and Clark* (Emigrant, MT, 2003), p. 48.

9 Apicius, *Cookery and Dining in Imperial Rome*, trans. Joseph Dommers Vehling (New York, 1977), p. 52.

10 Mark Shepard, *Restoration Agriculture* (Greeley, CO, 2013), p. 92.

11 *The Neapolitian Recipe Collection*, trans. Terence Scully (Ann Arbor, MI, 2000).

12 '110 Years of Fabbri Amarena', *Italian Tribune* (22 October 2014), www.italiantribune.com.

13 'National Pickle Day', www.holidayscalendar.com, accessed 12 December 2018.

14 Sherisse Pham, 'Warren Buffett Is the Face of Cherry Coke in China', www.money.cnn.com, 4 April 2017.

15 Adam Leith Gollner, *The Fruit Hunters* (New York, 2008), pp. 20–21.

16 Jane Grigson, *Jane Grigson's Fruit Book* (Lincoln, NE, 2007), p. 107.

17 'Céret Cherry Festival', www.southweststory.com, 22 May 2017.

18 Office de Tourisme Intercommunal, 'Monts de Venasque Cherry', www.ventoux-sud.com, accessed 12 December 2018.

19 'Kirazli Village – "Cherry Land"', www.kusadasigolfsparesort.com, accessed 12 December 2018.

20 'Cherry Stone Spitting – Greatest Distance', https://guinnessworldrecords.com, accessed 26 December 2018.

21 Jules Janick, ed., *Origin and Dissemination of Prunus Crops* (Hoboken, NJ, 2011), p. 68.

22 Malia Wollan, 'How to Knot a Cherry Stem with Your Tongue', *New York Times*, 23 June 2017.

4 Wood: Everlasting Beauty

1 Bob Dvorchak, 'Accident of Nature Turns Woodland Disaster into Profit', *Los Angeles Times* (19 April 1989).

2 Ibid.

3 Ibid.

4 Bailey Wood Products, 'Black Cherry (Appalachian Cherry)', www.baileywp.com, accessed 12 December 2018.

5 'Parlor Parquet Flooring', www.explorer.monticello.org, accessed 12 December 2018.

6 Charley Hannagan, 'Made in CNY: Harden Furniture Used by the White House', www.syracuse.com, 20 February 2012.

7 'Occasional Table: Noguchi Table', www.hermanmiller.com, accessed 12 December 2018.

8 Sanae Nakatani, 'George Nakashima', Densho Encyclopedia, www.encyclopedia.densho.org, 12 January 2018.

9 'Harpswell Arm Chair with Back', www.thosmoser.com, accessed 12 December 2018.

10 See www.trappistcaskets.com, accessed 12 December 2018.

11 Romanian Tourism Facebook, 'Romanian Spoons Tell the Stories of Life', 25 February 2010.

12 'Jonathan's Wild Cherry Spoons', www.woodspoon.com, accessed 12 December 2018.

13 National Museum of the American Indian, Collection Search catalogue #26/756, www.nmai.si.edu., accessed 12 December 2018.

14 'McClain's Printmaking Supplies, Cherry Plywood', www.imcclains.com, accessed 12 December 2018.

15 Marc Saumier, 'The Local Wood Challenge', www.marcsaumierluthier. com, 20 September 2018.

16 'Wand Wood Series Number Sixty Eight: Cherry', www.thecloveryone. tumblr.com, accessed 20 October 2019.

17 'Cherry Wood Magic Properties', www.wiccannaltar.com, accessed 12 December 2018.

18 Jane Hunter, *For the Love of an Orchard* (London, 2011), p. 179.

19 Robert and Mary Wilhelm, *A Ghostly Knight*, www.storyfest.com, accessed 27 December 2018.

20 'Touching History Pens and Gifts', www.histpens.com, accessed 12 December 2018.

21 'Cherry Bark Tea Canister', www.charaku-tea.com, accessed 12 December 2018.

22 Kelly Wetherille, 'A Japanese Craft Founded on Samurais and Cherry Trees', *New York Times*, Fashion Section, 3 November 2013.

23 'Tea Accessories', www.charaku-tea.com, accessed 12 December 2018.

24 Daniel Moerman, *Native American Food Plants: An Ethnobotanical Dictionary* (Portland, OR, 2010), p. 198.

25 '6 Benefits of Wild Cherry Bark', www.healthyfocus.org, accessed 12 December 2018.

26 'Kinnikinnick', www.herbcraft.org, accessed 12 December 2018.

27 'Uses of Cherry Tree Sap', www.hunker.com, accessed 12 December 2018.

28 Jan Timbrook, 'Use of Wild Cherry Pits as Food by the California Indians', *Journal of Ethnobiology*, 11/2 (December 1982), pp. 162–76.

29 Nicholas Culpeper, *Culpeper's Complete Herbal* (London, 1653), p. 45.

30 Richard Folkard, *Plant Lore, Legends and Lyrics* (London, 1884), p. 280.

31 'President Zachary Taylor Dies Unexpectedly', www.history.com, accessed 12 December 2018.

32 C. Frank Brockman, *Trees of North America* (New York, 2001), p. 166.

33 John Lindell, 'Cherry Tree Leaf Identification', www.hunker.com, accessed 16 April 2019.

34 'Diseases of the Weeping Cherry Tree', www.gardennet.com, accessed 16 April 2019.

35 Makiko Itoh, 'Cherry Blossom Captures the Flavor of Spring', *Japan Times* (23 March 2012).

5 Literature, Legend and Lore

1 Thomas Campion, 'There Is a Garden in Her Face' [1617], in *The Works of Thomas Campion*, ed. Water R. Davis (New York, 1970), p. 175.

2 Ehud Fathy, 'The Asàrotos òikos Mosaic as an Elite Status Symbol', PhD thesis, Tel Aviv University, 2017, p. 5.

3 Collection of the British Library, 'Roman de la Rosa', www.bl.uk/collection-items/roman-de-la-rose, accessed 12 December 2018.
4 Celia Fisher, *Flowers of the Renaissance* (London, 2011), p. 11.
5 Peter Glum, *The Key to Bosch's 'Garden of Earthly Delights' Found in Allegorical Bible Interpretation*, vol. 1 (Tokyo, 2007), p. 51.
6 Michael S. Beyer, *Bosch and Bruegel* (2000), at www.towerofbabel.com, accessed 12 December 2018.
7 Hans Belting, *Garden of Earthly Delights* (Munich, 2005), p. 7.
8 Metropolitan Museum of Art, collection description *The Holy Family*, at www.metmuseum.org/art/collection, accessed 12 December 2018.
9 'The Dutch Art Market in the Seventeenth Century', www.dutch.arts.gla.ac.uk, accessed 5 March 2019.
10 Jonathan Jones, 'Caravaggio and the Art of Dieting', *The Guardian* (28 May 2006), www.theguardian.com.
11 Ibid.
12 Ibid.
13 Margarita Russell, 'Iconography of Rembrandt's *Rape of Ganymede*', *Simiolus: Netherlands Quarterly for the History of Art*, IX/1 (1977).
14 Royal Museum of Fine Arts Antwerp, 'Kersen', www.kmska.be, accessed 12 December 2018.
15 P. R. Wilkinson, *Concise Thesaurus of English Metaphors* (London, 2007), p. 40.
16 Stephen Addis, Gerald Groemer and J. Thomas Rimer, eds, *Traditional Japanese Arts and Culture: An Illustrated Sourcebook* (Honolulu, HI, 2006), p. 48.
17 Halle Berry, www.azquotes.com, accessed 3 March 2019.
18 Curriculum Topic, Paul Cézanne, www.guggenheim.org, accessed 12 December 2018.
19 *Lesson: Rubber Stamping*, www.warhol.org/lessons/rubber-stamping, accessed 12 December 2018.
20 Debra Bass, 'Trademark is Cherry on Top of Iconic Dress', *St Louis Post Dispatch* (17 December 2016).
21 David Sheldon, 'How Fruit Machines Got Their Fruit Symbols', www.casino.org, 2013.
22 Amanda Arnold, 'Forbidden Fruit: Why Cherries are So Sexual', www.broadly.vice.com, 1 August 2016.
23 Armelle Sabatier, *Shakespeare and Visual Culture* (New York, 2016), p. 50.
24 Ibid.
25 Arnold, 'Forbidden Fruit'.
26 Jane Grigson, *Jane Grigson's Fruit Book* (London, 1982), p. 109.
27 See www.revolvy.com/page/Merryland, accessed 12 December 2018.
28 Sarah Toulalan, *Imagining Sex: Pornography and Bodies in Seventeenth-century England* (Oxford, 2007), p. 187.
29 Gordon Williams, *A Dictionary of Sexual Language and Imagery in Shakespeare and Stuart Literature*, vol. III (London, 2001), p. 233.
30 John Garfield, *The Wandering Whore*, numbers 1–5, 1660–1661, www.archives.org.

31 Arnold, 'Forbidden Fruit'.
32 Monique Truong, *The Book of Salt* (Boston, MA, 2004), p. 261.
33 'Cherry Tree Divination', www.magicherbal.blogspot.com,
    8 December 2006.
34 Thanh Sam, 'King of Pentacles', www.thanhsam30.worpress.com,
    accessed 12 December 2018.
35 'Cherry Magical Properties', www.eluneblue.com, accessed
    27 December 2018.
36 'Cherry-Mary and the Cherry Tree', www.herberowe.wordpress.com,
    accessed 3 March 2019.
37 Rebecca Buyer, 'The Folkloric Uses of Wood: Part V: Cherry',
    www.bloodandspicebush.com, accessed 3 March 2019.
38 'Barbarazweig', www.german-way.com, accessed 3 March 2019.
39 Mary Joan Winn Leith, 'The Origins of the Cherry Tree Carol',
    www.biblicalarchaeology.org, accessed 12 December 2018.
40 'I Gave My Love a Cherry', lyrics at www.songfacts.com, accessed
    12 December 2018.
41 'Soul Cake', lyrics at www.revolvy.com, accessed 12 December 2018.
42 Georg Frideric Handel, 'Acis and Galatea', lyrics at opera.stanford.edu,
    accessed 12 December 2018.
43 'Cherry Ripe', lyrics at www.bartleby.com, accessed 12 December 2018.
44 'Life is Just a Bowl of Cherries', lyrics at www.songfacts.com, accessed
    12 December 2018.
45 'Sweet Cherry Wine', lyrics at www.songfacts.com, accessed
    12 December 2018.

6 The Future of Cherries

1 Emma Cowing, 'Raspberries in Decline as Blueberry Demand Soars',
   The Scotsman (8 September 2013), www.scotsman.com.
2 'Observations from Carandale Farm, Meader Bush Cherry',
   www.uncommonfruit.cias.wisc.edu, accessed 12 December 2018.
3 G. Gradinariu, 'New Cherry Cultivars and Hybrids Created at IASI
   Fruit Research Station, Romania', International Society for Horticulture
   Science, 2008, www.ishs.org, accessed 12 December 2018.
4 'Research on Cherry Blossom Trees', www.newvoicesforresearch.
   blogspot.com, 1 April 2009.
5 'Japanese Scientists Create Cherry Tree that Blooms all Year Round',
   The Telegraph (17 February 2010), www.telegraph.co.uk.

Select Bibliography

Abe, Naoko, *'Cherry' Ingram: The Englishman Who Saved Japan's Blossoms*
  (London, 2019)
Badenes, Maria Luisa, and David H. Byrne, eds, *Fruit Breeders*
  (New York, 2012)
Bader, Myles H., *Cherry Creations: The Ultimate Cherry Cookbook*
  (Las Vegas, NV, 1995)
Barter, Judith, ed., *Art and Appetite: American Painting, Culture, and Cuisine*
  (Chicago, IL, 2013)
Bowden, Lindsay, *Damn Fine Cherry Pie* (New York, 2016)
Brockman, C. Frank, *Trees of North America* (New York, 2001)
Gollner, Adam, *The Fruit Hunters* (New York, 2008)
Gosalbo, Laura and Gerard Solis, *Crazy about Cherries* (Gretna, LA, 2009)
Grigson, Jane, *Jane Grigson's Fruit Book* (London, 1982)
Holland, Leandra, *Feasting and Fasting with Lewis and Clark: A Food and Social History
  of the Early 1800s* (Emigrant, MT, 2003)
Hunter, Jane McMorland, *For the Love of an Orchard* (London, 2011)
Janick, Jules, ed., *Origin and Dissemination of Prunus Crops: Peach, Cherry, Apricot,
  Plum, Almond* (New York, 1997)
Kuitert, Wybe, *Japanese Flowering Cherries* (Portland, OR, 1999)
Malaguzzi, Silvia, *Food and Feasting in Art* (Milan, 2006)
Musgrave, Toby, and Clay Perry, *Heirloom Fruits and Vegetables* (New York, 2012)
Nims, Cynthia, *Stone Fruit* (Portland, OR, 2003)
Palter, Robert, *The Duchess of Malfi's Apricots, and Other Literary Fruits*
  (Columbia, SC, 2002)
Pauly, Philip, *Fruits and Plains: The Horticultural Transformation of America*
  (Cambridge, MA, 2007)
Riley, Gillian, *Food in Art from Prehistory to the Renaissance* (London, 2015)
Skinner, Charles, *Myths and Legends of Flowers, Trees, Fruits, and Plants*
  (Philadelphia, PA, 2011)
Toussaint-Samat, Maguelonne, *A History of Food* (Cambridge, MA, 1992)

Associations and Websites

Farm and Orchard Information

The following websites will help the reader to think about ways they too can experience more fresh cherries through community gardens and farm tours:

FALLEN FRUIT

A collaboration of activist artists promoting the planting of fruit trees and the harvesting of fruit on public land.
www.fallenfruit.org

PHILADELPHIA ORCHARD PROJECT

Works with community-based groups to plan and plant orchards in the city.
www.phillyorchards.org

COTEHELE

The farm on this estate in Cornwall, UK, has a mother orchard that protects and archives local fruit varieties that might otherwise not be propagated in the area.
www.nationaltrust.org.uk/Cotehele

ANDY'S ORCHARD

Andy's Orchard, in Morgan Hill, California, has forty different varieties of rare, modern hybrids and heirloom varieties.
https://andysorchard.com

RENT A CHERRY TREE

A Kent farm that allows renting a cherry tree on an annual basis for owners to harvest the crop themselves.
www.rentacherrytree.co.uk

Cherry Products

The websites below offer the reader examples of the many cherry products
that can be purchased online:

CHERRY REPUBLIC

A unique store selling only products containing cherries locally grown in
Michigan – includes such items as cherry sausage, chutney, salsas, etc.
www.cherryrepublic.com

KALUSTYAN'S

A speciality food store in New York City featuring unique cherry products
such as mahlab and cherry bark and leaf teas.
www.kalustyan.org

VERMONT HARDWOOD PENS

Maker of pens using reclaimed wood, including cherry wood.
https://vermonthardwoodpens.com

HEIRLOOM GIFT PENS

Cherry wood gifts made of wood from historic sites.
www.etsy.com/shop/heimloomgiftpens

CHUKAR CHERRIES

Premium cherry products including chocolates and locally grown cherries
from the state of Washington.
www.chukar.com

NIHON AND ICHIBON: JAPANS BEST TO YOU

Offers a wide selection of edible *sakura* cherry blossom products.
www.anythingfromjapan.com

CHERRY BOMBE

A biannual publication, a weekly radio podcast and a Cherry Jubilee
conference.
www.cherrybombe.com

Festivals

Festivals and county and country fairs are a good way to taste fresh, local
cherries and have fun!

NATIONAL CHERRY AND SOFT FRUIT SHOW

An annual event at the Kent County Show in July, which exhibits the best
cherries grown in the county of Kent, England.
www.ncsfs.co.uk

Associations and Websites

NATIONAL CHERRY BLOSSOM FESTIVAL
An annual spring celebration in Washington, DC, commemorating the 1912
gift of Japanese cherry trees to the U.S.
www.nationalcherryblossomfestival.org

FESTIVAL DE LA CERISE ET DU TERROIR (CHERRY FESTIVAL AT VENASQUE)
An annual cherry harvest festival in Venasque, France, sponsored by the
Brotherhood of the Cherry of Mont de Venasque.
www.tourisme-venasque.com

FESTA DA CEREJA (CHERRY FESTIVAL)
The centre of the cherry route and location of the annual festival for the
cherry-growing region in Portugal.
www.portugalvisitor.com

CHERRY FESTIVAL PECETTO TORINESE, ITALY
A cherry harvest festival with community celebrations, including parades in
historic costumes.
www.turinspots.com/cherry-festival

NATIONAL CHERRY FESTIVAL
Oldest and largest cherry festival in the U.S.; takes places annually in Traverse
City, Michigan, in July.
www.cherryfestival.org

FÊTE DE LA CERISE EN CÉRET (CÉRET CHERRY FESTIVAL)
A festival held annually in May, celebrating the earliest cherry harvest in France.
www.en.destinationsudde.france.com

CHERRY FESTIVAL SEFROU
A UNESCO Intangible World Heritage celebration in Sefrou, Morocco.
www.morocco.com

YouTube Videos

Some things are better seen than described. The following links to YouTube
videos should be interesting and fun.

DIY CHERRY PITTERS
www.youtube.com/watch?v=LevzJ7X1A_Q
www.youtube.com/watch?v=19Z2T2ECyZA

MECHANICAL CHERRY HARVESTING
www.youtube.com/watch?v=ykGuOIMGbLI

TYING A CHERRY STEM INTO A KNOT
www.youtube.com/watch?v=OASzBeIRiHo

MAKING CHOCOLATE-COVERED CHERRIES
www.youtube.com/watch?v=sUpZGfNPRUY

WILD CHERRY TREES AND CATTLE SAFETY
www.youtube.com/watch?v=KmAQIIiWAWY

Acknowledgements

We are grateful to the many people who shared their knowledge of cherry with us, and helped us along the way.

We would like to thank English orchardist James Evans and his wife Mary Martin, and, in Romania, Dr Mihail Coman at the European Commission Research Institute for Fruit Growing Piteşti. A special thanks to Vera Keleman, the Reverend Hegedus Tivador and the people of Szentlaszlo Unitarian Universalist Church in Romania for their hospitality. They shared cherry recipes, food and songs with us, and we dedicated and planted a cherry tree at their church.

Novelist Irene Zabytko helped guide us in Ukraine, and took us to her cousin's cherry orchard outside Lviv. Nicolau Andresen, Cultural Affairs Attaché at the u.s. Embassy in Lisbon, Portugal, connected us to tourist offices in the cherry-growing regions of the country. Marta Serra at the Office of Tourism Fundão in Portugal was an invaluable aide to our research.

Our thanks to photographer and friend Joanne Bening. Thanks to Paula Roberts who shared with us cherry-related products from Japan. We can't forget our family and friends who participated in our cherry picnic, played cherry games, and tasted cherry recipes; special thanks to Peter Okin for his cherry-wood barbecue.

Dr Kathryn Lorenz of Lorenz Language Consultants was an early reader of the book and gave us editing and proofreading assistance, as did the Friends and Books book club in Cincinnati. Our thanks also to Dr Charles Seibert and Dr Lowanne Jones for their expertise in philosophy and art. Horticulturalists Richard and Nenya Milne provided useful comments and edits.

We wish to thank the wonderful staff at the St Bernard Branch of the Cincinnati and Hamilton County Public Library, and the staff at the library of Pennsylvania State University, Brandywine Campus. Susan H. Fugate, Head of Collection Management and Special Collections, u.s. Department of Agriculture (usda) National Agricultural Library, and her professional staff provided fascinating and rare research materials.

We wish to show our gratitude to our mother, Doris Watson, and to Phil Forsyth, Executive Director of the Philadelphia Orchard Project, who helped arrange a cherry tree planting in her memory in a Philadelphia urban garden.

Photo Acknowledgements

The author and publishers wish to express their thanks to the following sources of illustrative material and/or permission to reproduce it. Some locations are also supplied here for reasons of brevity.

Photo courtesy of 3 Cats Studio: p. 68; Amon Carter Museum of American Art, Fort Worth: p. 161; British Library, London: p. 15; photo Chef's Garden: p. 173; Christ College, Oxford Picture Gallery: p. 138; Gemäldegalerie Alte Meister, Dresden: p. 145; Greater Loveland Historical Society Museum, Loveland, Ohio: p. 103; Historisches Museum, Frankfurt (on loan to the Städel Museum, Frankfurt): p. 133 (top); collection of Constance Kirker: pp. 18, 43, 50, 120, 131, 163; photos Constance Kirker: pp. 9, 10, 18, 20, 22, 23, 27, 28, 29, 30, 31, 34, 35, 39, 43, 46, 50, 56, 59, 64, 70, 72, 76, 77, 78, 81, 82, 84, 85, 86, 88, 89, 90, 92, 93, 94, 95, 96, 101, 102, 107, 111, 112, 114, 115, 117, 120, 121, 122, 126, 127, 131, 132, 154, 155, 163, 169, 174, 176; Kunsthistorisches Museum Vienna: p. 140; Library of Congress, Washington, DC (Prints and Photographs Division): p. 79; Los Angeles County Museum of Art (Open Access): p. 151; Medici Villa and Still Life Museum, Florence, photo Universal Images Group/SuperStock: p. 17; Metropolitan Museum of Art (Open Access): pp. 52–3, 55, 108, 134, 139, 158; courtesy Thomas Moser: p. 113; Musée d'Orsay, Paris: p. 150; Museo del Prado, Madrid: p. 135; Museum of Fine Arts, Boston, Massachusetts: p. 69; photo NASA/ Bill Ingalls: p. 110; National Gallery, London: pp. 136, 137, 143; photo Jim Nugeot: p. 172; Planes of Fame Museum, Chino, California: p. 54; private collections: pp. 133 (foot), 141, 147, 149; Skokloster Castle, Sweden: p. 130; State Hermitage Museum, Saint Petersburg: p. 146; Toledo Museum of Art, Ohio: p. 128; U.S. Department of Agriculture National Agricultural Library, Beltsville, Maryland (Pomological Watercolor collection): pp. 12, 21, 25, 32; Vatican Museums, Rome: p. 15; photo Walker Art Center, Minneapolis/Minneapolis Park and Recreation Board: p. 153; courtesy of the artist (Amy Yosmali): p. 152.

Index

Page numbers in *italics* refer to illustrations;
numbers in **bold** refer to recipes.